VOGUE® KNITTING
BAGSTWO

VOGUE® KNITTING
BAGSTWO

SIXTH&SPRING BOOKS
NEW YORK

SIXTH&SPRING BOOKS
233 Spring Street
New York, New York 10013

Library of Congress Cataloging-in-Publication Data

Library of Congress Control Number: 2006931204
ISBN: 1-933027-09-6
ISBN-13: 978-1-933027-09-8

Manufactured in China

1 3 5 7 9 10 8 6 4 2

First Edition
2007

TABLE OF CONTENTS

INTRODUCTION

For almost any woman, the handbag is the ultimate accessory. It combines fashion and function and suggests couture in a beautifully useful package. A fabulous bag has a unique way of grabbing people's attention—think of it as having the same effect as a sports car with (in most cases) a much lower price tag.

In *Bags Two* you will find a wealth of patterns to knit and adore. When you are getting ready to hit the town, the Evening Bag on p. 46, made of gorgeous silk yarn, will be an eye-catching companion. The felted Weekender Bag (p. 28) will inspire you to take a road trip, if only to show it off! And for everyday carryalls, the Cabled Shoulder Bag on p. 25 is a luscious choice for winter, while the Freeform Bag on p. 74 makes a delightful piece for summer.

You will find bags to make that you didn't even know you needed. The Market Bag on p. 64 is perfect for picking up your fruits and veggies, and keep your Bottle Bag (p. 90) on hand to help you get in your eight glasses of water a day.

With the impressive quality and variety of hardware available, bag patterns have never been more fun. In designing these bags we have tried to take full advantage of the beautiful handles and clasps available, and we have provided resources for where to purchase them.

So gather your yarn and accoutrements, pick a bag, any bag, and get ready to **KNIT ON THE GO!**

THE BASICS

Handbags, purses, backpacks, totes, pouches—one thing is for sure, a woman never leaves home without one of them. Whether your bag holds your wallet and a few grooming necessities or acts as a small suitcase, the handbag you choose to carry is probably one of the most important accessories in your wardrobe.

On the following pages you'll find a variety of bags to fit every taste, season, age and mood—not to mention skill level.

You'll find a wide assortment of shapes and sizes suitable for everything from a trip to the beach to a night on the town. Many of the larger totes can double as wonderful knitting bags—a unique way to carry your on-the-go projects.

STRUCTURE OF BAGS AND BACKPACKS

Knitting a bag is a simple undertaking. Many of the designs in this collection are based on squares or rectangles—think of it as knitting a large-scale swatch with some finishing. Most have a single- or double-fold flap with a loop and button or other closure—some even sport ribbon ties and buckles.

Other bags have side gussets to add width to the inside of the bag. In some cases the gussets may continue on to become straps; in others, separate straps are sewn on. There are also several designs with envelope-style flaps with a V- or U-shaped styling.

Some of the bags are styled as pouches with oval or circular bottoms and straight sides. The circular bottoms are knit from the center outward on double pointed needles or picked up from the sides of the bag and worked inward to the center.

Several of the bags are finished with purchased ready-made plastic or wooden handles, and trimmed with beads and buttons, or appliqués for handy usage or decoration. There are also a few backpacks in this book with two-strap shoulder styling.

BAG FABRIC

Unlike most other knitting projects, bags require a firm fabric. This can be accom-

GAUGE

It is always important to knit a gauge swatch, and it is even more so with garments to ensure proper fit.

Patterns usually state gauge over a 4"/10cm span; however, it's beneficial to make a larger test swatch. This gives a more precise stitch gauge, a better idea of the appearance and drape of the knitted fabric, and a chance for you to familiarize yourself with the stitch pattern.

The type of needles used—straight or double pointed, wood or metal—will influence gauge, so knit your swatch with the needles you plan to use for the project. Measure gauge as illustrated. Try different needle sizes until your sample measures the required number of stitches and rows. *To get fewer stitches to the inch/cm, use larger needles; to get more stitches to the inch/cm, use smaller needles.*

Knitting in the round may tighten the gauge, so if you measured the gauge on a flat swatch, take another gauge reading after you begin knitting. When the piece measures at least 2"/5cm, lay it flat and measure over the stitches in the center of the piece, as the side stitches may be distorted.

It's a good idea to keep your gauge swatch in order to test blocking and cleaning methods.

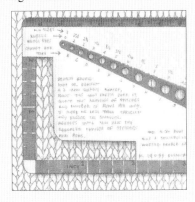

plished by working in a tighter gauge than average for the particular yarn. To achieve a tighter gauge, knit with needles that are two or three sizes smaller than is recommended on the ball band.

Another method is to felt the knitted bag, as we have done with several of our bags, such as the Felted Diamond Bag on page 53. The combination of hot water and agitation from the washing machine solidifies the fabric, and gives added structure.

YARN SELECTION

For an exact reproduction of the bag photographed, use the yarn listed in the Materials section of the pattern. We've selected yarns that are readily available in the U.S. and Canada at the time of printing. The Resources list in the back of the book provides addresses of yarn distributors.

Contact them for the name of a retailer in your area.

YARN SUBSTITUTION

You may wish to substitute yarns. Perhaps you have a spectacular yarn you've been dying to try, maybe you view small-scale projects as a chance to incorporate leftovers from your yarn stash, or the yarn specified may not be available in your area. Bags allow you to be creative, but you'll need to knit to the given gauge to obtain the knitted measurements with the substitute yarn (see Gauge on the previous page). Make pattern adjustments where necessary. Be sure to consider how different yarn types (chenille, mohair, bouclé, etc.) will affect the final appearance of your bag.

Some of the most common fibers used for bags are acrylics or blends for washability, rayon or rayon blends for durability and strength. If you plan to felt your bag it is best to use 100% wool or wool blended with alpaca, mohair or cashmere.

To facilitate yarn substitution, Vogue Knitting grades yarn by the standard stitch gauge obtained in stockinette stitch. You'll find a grading number in the Materials section of the pattern, immediately following the fiber type of the yarn. Look for a substitute yarn that falls into the same category. The suggested needle size and gauge on the ball band should be comparable to that on the Yarn Symbols chart opposite.

After you've successfully gauge-swatched a substitute yarn, you'll need to figure out how much of the substitute yarn the project requires. First, find the total length of the original yarn in the pattern (multiply number of balls by yards/meters per ball). Divide this figure by the new yards/meters per ball (listed on the ball band). Round up to the next whole number. This is the number of balls required to knit your project.

FOLLOWING CHARTS

Charts provide a convenient way to follow colorwork, lace, cable and other stitch patterns at a glance. Vogue Knitting stitch charts utilize the universal knitting language of "symbolcraft." Unless otherwise indicated, read charts from right to left on right side (RS) rows, and from left to right on wrong side (WS) rows, repeating any stitch and row repeats as directed in the pattern. Posting a self-adhesive note under your working row is an easy way to keep track of your place on a chart.

COLORWORK KNITTING

Two main types of colorwork are explored in this book.

Categories of yarn, gauge ranges, and recommended needle and hook sizes

Yarn Weight Symbol & Category Names	1 Super Fine	2 Fine	3 Light	4 Medium	5 Bulky	6 Super Bulky
Type of Yarns in Category	Sock, Fingering, Baby	Sport, Baby	DK, Light Worsted	Worsted, Afghan, Aran	Chunky, Craft, Rug	Bulky, Roving
Knit Gauge Range* in Stockinette Stitch to 4 Inches	27–32 sts	23–26 sts	21–24 sts	16–20 sts	12–15 sts	6–11 sts
Recommended Needle in Metric Size Range	2.25–3.25 mm	3.25–3.75 mm	3.75–4.5 mm	4.5–5.5 mm	5.5–8 mm	8 mm and larger
Recommended Needle U.S. Size Range	1 to 3	3 to 5	5 to 7	7 to 9	9 to 11	11 and larger
Crochet Gauge* Ranges in Single Crochet To 4 Inch	21–32 sts	16–20 sts	12–17 sts	11–14 sts	8–11 sts	5–9 sts
Recommended Hook in Metric Size Range	2.25–3.5 mm	3.5–4.5 mm	4.5–5.5 mm	5.5–6.5 mm	6.5–9 mm	9 mm and larger
Recommended Hook U.S. Size Range	B–1 to E–4	E–4 to 7	7 to I–9	I–9 to K–10½	K–10½ to M–13	M–13 and larger

*Guidelines only: The above reflects the most commonly used needle or hook sizes for specific yarn categories.

■□□□
Beginner
Ideal first project.

■■□□
Very Easy Very Vogue
Basic stitches, minimal shaping, simple finishing.

■■■□
Intermediate
For knitters with some experience. More intricate stitches, shaping and finishing.

■■■■
Experienced
For knitters able to work patterns with complicated shaping and finishing.

There are different ways to make a yarn over. Which method to use depends on where you are in the stitch pattern. If you do not make the yarn over in the right way, you may lose it on the following row, or make a yarn over that is too big. Here are the different variations:

Between two knit stitches: Bring the yarn from the back of the work to the front between the two needles. Knit the next stitch, bringing the yarn to the back over the right-hand needle, as shown.

Between a knit and a purl stitch: Bring the yarn from the back to the front between the two needles. Then bring it to the back over the right-hand needle and back to the front again, as shown. Purl the next stitch.

Between a purl and a knit stitch: Leave the yarn at the front of the work. Knit the next stitch, bringing the yarn to the back over the right-hand needle, as shown.

Between two purl stitches: Leave the yarn at the front of the work. Bring the yarn to the back over the right-hand needle and to the front again, as shown. Purl the next stitch.

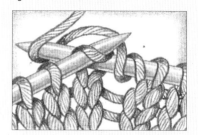

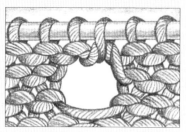

Multiple yarn overs (two or more): Wrap the yarn around the needle, as when working a single yarn over, then continue wrapping the yarn around the needle as many times as indicated. Work the next stitch of the left-hand needle. On the following row, work stitches into the extra yarn overs as described in the pattern. The illustration at right depicts a finished yarn-over on the purl side.

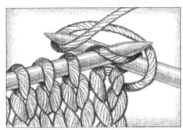

At the beginning of a knit row: Insert the right-hand needle knitwise into the first stitch on the left-hand needle, keeping the yarn in front of the needle. Bring the yarn over the right-hand needle to the back and knit the first stitch, holding the yarn over with your thumb if necessary.

At the beginning of a purl row: Insert the right-hand needle purlwise into the first stitch on the left-hand needle, keeping the yarn behind the needle. Purl the first stitch.

Intarsia

Intarsia is accomplished with separate bobbins of individual colors. This method is ideal for large blocks of color or for motifs that aren't repeated close together. When changing colors, always pick up the new color and wrap it around the old color to prevent holes.

Stranding

When motifs are closely placed, color-work is accomplished by stranding along two or more colors per row, creating "floats" on the wrong side of the fabric. When using this method, twist yarns on WS to prevent holes and strand loosely to keep knitting from puckering.

Note that yarn amounts have been calculated for the colorwork method suggested in the pattern. Knitting a stranded pattern with intarsia bobbins will take less yarn, while stranding an intarsia pattern will require more yarn.

BLOCKING

Blocking is the best way to shape pattern pieces and smooth knitted edges. However, some yarns, such as chenilles and ribbons, do not benefit from blocking. Choose a blocking method using information on the yarn care label and, when in doubt, test-block your gauge swatch.

Wet Block Method

Using rustproof pins, pin the finished bag to measurements on a flat surface and lightly dampen using a spray bottle. Allow to dry before removing the pins.

Steam Block Method

Pin the finished bag to measurements with the wrong side of the knitting facing up. Steam lightly, holding the iron 2"/5cm

CIRCULAR NEEDLES

Hold the needle tip with the last cast-on stitch in your right hand and the tip with the first cast-on stitch in your left hand. Knit the first cast-on stitch, pulling the yarn tight to avoid a gap.

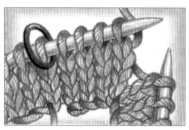

Work until you reach the marker. This completes the first round. Slip the marker to the right needle and work the next round.

TWISTED CORD

1 If you have someone to help you, insert a pencil or knitting needle through each end of the strands. If not, place one end over a doorknob and put a pencil through the other end. Turn the strands clockwise until they are tightly twisted.

2 Keeping the strands taut, fold the piece in half. Remove the pencils and allow the cords to twist onto themselves.

DOUBLE POINTED NEEDLES

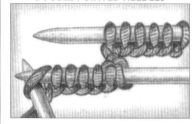

1 Cast on the required number of stitches on the first needle, plus one extra. Slip this extra stitch to the next needle as shown. Continue in this way, casting on the required number of stitches on the last needle.

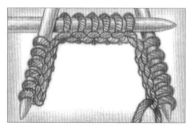

2 Arrange the needles as shown, with the cast-on edge facing the center of the triangle (or square).

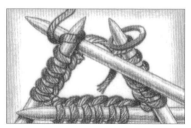

3 Place a stitch marker after the last cast-on stitch. With the free needle, knit the first cast-on stitch, pulling the yarn tightly. Continue knitting in rounds, slipping the marker before beginning each round.

above the work. Do not press the iron onto the knitting, as it will flatten the stitches. This is the better method to use for bags knit in one piece. If you cannot pin the bag flat, simply steam it on the end of an ironing board.

ASSEMBLY

Most bags are knit in one piece. Some are made circularly, therefore no seaming is required. Some are made in squares or rectangles, then folded in half with side seams. Some bags have a separate gusset that is sewn between the front and back pieces.

Seaming can be done using any of these methods:

1. Sewing, using the traditional seaming method used for sweaters.

2. Sewing from the right side, leaving one or two edge stitches free for a decorative ridge.

3. Crocheting, using either slip stitch or single crochet.

4. Embroidery after seaming, using a decorative stitch such as cross stitch or herringbone, as we did in our Felted Clutch on page 43.

LINING

Adding a fabric lining to your bag has several advantages. It hides the sometimes unfinished look of the "wrong side" of the knitting, adds strength, and can create an interesting design element. The best fabrics to use are washable woven fabrics such as broadcloth, silk or felt. Use the knitted bag as a template to cut out the fabric, adding a ½"/1.25cm seam allowance on all sides. Sew the pieces together as you did for the knitted pieces. With wrong sides together, place the sewn fabric inside the knitted band, turn down the top edge and slip stitch it in place.

CARE

Refer to the yarn label for the recommended cleaning method. Many of the bags in the book can be washed either by hand or in the machine on a gentle or wool cycle, in lukewarm water with a mild detergent. Do not agitate, and don't soak for more than 10 minutes. Rinse gently with tepid water, then fold in a towel and gently press the water out. Lay flat to dry away from excess heat and light. Check the yarn band for any specific care instructions such as dry cleaning or tumble drying.

DUPLICATE STITCH

Duplicate stitch covers a knit stitch. Bring the needle up below the stitch to be worked. Insert the needle under both loops one row above and pull it through. Insert it back into the stitch below and through the center of the next stitch in one motion, as shown.

THE KITCHENER STITCH

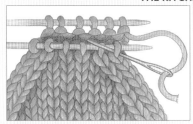
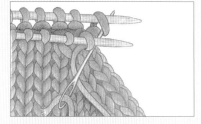

1 Insert tapestry needle purlwise (as shown) through first stitch on front needle. Pull yarn through, leaving that stitch on knitting needle.

2 Insert tapestry needle knitwise (as shown) through first stitch on back needle. Pull yarn through, leaving stitch on knitting needle.

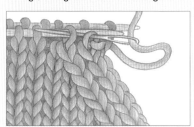
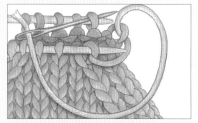

3 Insert tapestry needle knitwise through first stitch on front needle, slip stitch off needle and insert tapestry needle purlwise (as shown) through next stitch on front needle. Pull yarn through, leaving this stitch on needle.

4 Insert tapestry needle purlwise through first stitch on back needle. Slip stitch off needle and insert tapestry needle knitwise (as shown) through next stitch on back needle. Pull yarn through, leaving this stitch on needle.
Repeat steps 3 and 4 until all stitches on both front and back needles have been grafted. Fasten off and weave in end.

KNITTING TERMS AND ABBREVIATIONS

approx approximately

beg begin(ning)

bind off Used to finish an edge and keep stitches from unraveling. Lift the first stitch over the second, the second over the third, etc. (U.K.: cast off)

cast on A foundation row of stitches placed on the needle in order to begin knitting.

CC contrast color

ch chain(s)

cm centimeter(s)

cn cable needle

cont continu(e)(ing)

dc double crochet (U.K.: tr–treble)

dec decrease(ing)—Reduce the stitches in a row (knit 2 together).

dpn double pointed needle(s)

foll follow(s)(ing)

g gram(s)

garter stitch Knit every row. Circular knitting: Knit one round, then purl one round.

hdc half-double crochet (U.K.: htr–half treble)

inc increase(ing)—Add stitches in a row (knit into the front and back of a stitch).

k knit

k f & b knit into front and back of stitch

k2tog knit 2 stitches together

lp(s) loops(s)

LH left-hand

m meter(s)

M1 make one stitch—With the needle tip, lift the strand between last stitch worked and next stitch on the left-hand needle and knit into the back of it. One stitch has been added.

MC main color

mm millimeter(s)

oz ounce(s)

p purl

p2tog purl 2 stitches together

pat pattern

pick up and knit (purl) Knit (or purl) into the loops along an edge.

pm place marker—Place or attach a loop of contrast yarn or purchased stitch marker as indicated.

psso pass slip stitch over

rem remain(s)(ing)

rep repeat

rev St st reverse Stockinette stitch—Purl right-side rows, knit wrong-side rows. Circular knitting: Purl all rounds. (U.K.: reverse stocking stitch)

rnd(s) round(s)

RH right-hand

RS right side(s)

sc single crochet (U.K.: dc–double crochet)

sk skip

SKP Slip 1, knit 1, pass slip stitch over knit 1.

SK2P Slip 1, knit 2 together, pass slip stitch over k2tog.

sl slip—An unworked stitch made by passing a stitch from the left-hand to the right-hand needle as if to purl.

sl st slip stitch (U.K.: single crochet)

ssk slip, slip, knit—Slip next 2 stitches knitwise, one at a time, to right-hand needle. Insert tip of left-hand needle into fronts of these stitches from left to right. Knit them together. One stitch has been decreased.

st(s) stitch(es)

St st Stockinette stitch—Knit right-side rows, purl wrong-side rows. Circular knitting: Knit all rounds. (U.K.: stocking stitch)

tbl through back of loop

tog together

tr treble crochet (U.K.: dtr–double treble)

WS wrong side(s)

w&t wrap and turn

wyif with yarn in front

wyib with yarn in back

work even Continue in pattern without increasing or decreasing. (U.K.: work straight)

yd yard(s)

yo yarn over—Make a new stitch by wrapping the yarn over the right-hand needle. (U.K.: yfwd, yon, yrn)

* Repeat directions following * as many times as indicated.

[ ] Repeat directions inside brackets as many times as indicated.

MESSENGER BAG
Carpetbagger

Easy-to-work slip stitches give a woven appearance to this generously sized bag with zipper. The long strap extends from the sides, making it easy to sling over your shoulder. Designed by Jeannie Chin.

KNITTED MEASUREMENTS

■ Approx 12"/30.5cm wide x 10"/25.5cm high (excluding strap)

MATERIALS

■ 4 1¾oz/50g balls (each approx 55yd/ 50m) of Classic Elite Yarns *Paintbox* (wool) in #6849 pacific island (5)

■ One pair each sizes 9 and 10 (5.5 and 6mm) needles *or size to obtain gauge*

■ Zipper 12"/30.5cm long

GAUGE

20 sts and 37 rows to 4"/10cm over double fabric st using larger needles.
Take time to check gauge.

STITCH GLOSSARY

S2KP Slip 2 sts knitwise, k1, pass 2 slip sts over the k1.

DOUBLE FABRIC STITCH

(multiple of 4 sts)
Row 1 (RS) K1, *sl 2 wyif, k2; rep from *, end sl 2 wyif, k1.
Row 2 K1, p2, *sl 2 wyib, p2; rep from *, end k1.
Rep rows 1 and 2 for double fabric st.

BACK

Beg at top edge, with smaller needles, cast on 60 sts. K 1 row. Change to larger needles and work in double fabric st until piece measures 9"/25cm from beg, end with WS row.

Bottom shaping

Next (dec) row (RS) S2KP, *k2tog, sl 2 wyif; rep from *, end k2tog, k3tog—42 sts.
Next (bind off) row K1, sl 1 wyib, bind off, *[p1, bind off] twice, sl 1 wyib, bind off; rep from *, end k1, bind off.

FRONT

Work as for back.

GUSSET/STRAP

With larger needles, cast on 8 sts.
Row 1 (RS) K1, sl 2 wyif, k2, sl 2 wyif, k1.
Row 2 K1, p2, sl 2 wyib, p2, k1.
Rep rows 1 and 2 until piece measures 75"/190.5cm from beg. Bind off in pat st.

FINISHING

Block pieces to measurements. Sew short ends of gusset/strap tog. Center gusset/strap seam on center bottom edge of bag back. Whipstitch gusset in place. Rep on bag front. Baste zipper in place. Sew in zipper.

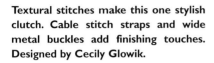

Textural stitches make this one stylish clutch. Cable stitch straps and wide metal buckles add finishing touches. Designed by Cecily Glowik.

KNITTED MEASUREMENTS
■ Approx 10"/25.5cm wide x 4¾"/125cm high

MATERIALS
■ 2 1¾oz/50g balls (each approx 109yd/100m) of Cascade Yarns *Pima Silk* (cotton/silk) in #5144 olive 🔲
■ One pair size 6 (4mm) needles *or size to obtain gauge*
■ Two 1⅛"/3cm wide Dritz fashion buckles #150-65
■ ½yd/.5m lining fabric, sewing needle, thread to match

GAUGE
24 sts and 28 rows to 4"/10cm over diagonal scallop pat using size 6 (4mm) needles.
Take time to check gauge.

Notes
1 Bag is made in one piece.
2 Straps are made separately and sewn on.

DIAGONAL SCALLOP PATTERN
(multiple of 4 sts plus 2)
Rows 1 and 3 (WS) Purl.
Row 2 K1, *insert needle from behind and lift the strand between the last st worked and the next st on LH needle, k2, then pass the strand over the 2 sts, k2; rep from *, end k1.

Row 4 K3, *insert needle from behind and lift the strand between the last st worked and the next st on LH needle, k2, then pass the strand over the 2 sts, k2; rep from *, end last rep k1.
Rep rows 1 to 4 for diagonal scallop pat.

SLIP STITCH CABLE
(worked over 10 sts)
Row 1 (WS) K2, p6, k2.
Rows 2 and 4 P2, sl 1 wyib, k4, sl 1 wyib, p2.
Rows 3 and 5 K2, sl 1 wyif, p4, sl 1 wyif, k2.
Row 6 P2, drop sl-st off needle to front of work, k2, then pick up sl-st and knit it (take care not to twist sl-st), sl next 2 sts to RH needle, drop next sl-st off needle to front of work, then sl the 2 sts back to left-hand needle, pick up dropped st with RH needle, replace it on the LH needle and knit it, k2, p2.
Rep rows 1 to 6 for slip st cable.

BAG
Cast on 58 sts. Work in St st for ¾"/2cm, end with a WS row. Purl next row on RS for turning ridge. Cont in diagonal scallop pat until piece measures 11"/28cm from

turning ridge, end with row 4. K next row on WS for turning ridge. Cont in St st for ¾"/2cm. Bind off.

STRAPS
(make 2)
Cast on 10 sts. Work in slip st cable for 14"/35.5cm. Bind off.

FINISHING
Block piece to measurements. Using bag as a template, cut out fabric lining ½"/1.3cm larger all around than bag. Turn fabric lining seam allowance ½"/1.3cm to WS; press. Slip stitch edge of lining to WS of bag. Fold purse hem to WS at each turning ridge and sew in place.

With RS facing, position straps 1¾"/4.5cm in from each side edge, with ends extending 3"/7.5cm above bound-off edge of bag; pin in place. At opposite end of each strap, place center of buckle under a strap, with prong through strap at 2½"/6.5cm from cast-on edge of bag and making sure that prong points toward top edge of bag; pin in place. Sew edge straps in place. With WS facing, fold cast-on edge up 4½"/11.5cm, leaving 2"/5cm free for flap. Sew side seams; turn right side out. Buckle straps.

Cabled blue persuasion

One big cable creates the center focus on this slouchy shoulder bag. It's the perfect introduction to making cables. Designed by Christa Tegtmeier.

6-ST CABLE

Row 1 (RS) K6.
Row 2 P6.
Row 3 Sl 3 sts to cn and hold to front, k3, k3 from cn.
Rows 4, 6 and 8 P6.
Rows 5, 7 and 9 K6.
Row 10 P6.
Rep rows 1 to 10 for 6-st cable.

BACK

Cast on 38 sts.
Beg cable pat
Row 1 (RS) K8, p2, k3, p3, work 6-st cable, p3, k3, p2, k8. Row 2 P8, k2, p3, k3, work 6-st cable, k3, p3, k2, p8. Cont to work in this way until piece measures 16"/40.5cm from beg, end with a WS row.
Next row (RS) K8 and place these sts on holder for strap, k22, place rem 8 sts on holder for strap. Beg with a p row, work in St st over center 22 sts for 2"/5cm for facing. Bind off.

FRONT

Work as for back.

FINISHING

Block pieces to measurements. Sew side and bottom seams.

Strap

With RS facing, k 8 sts from left back holder and 8 sts from right front holder—16 sts. Beg with a p row, work in St st for 20"/51cm. Bind off. Rep for other side of strap.

Lining

Fold lining fabric in half, RS facing. Trace body of bag onto lining fabric. Cut out pieces ½"/1.3cm larger all around. Using a ½"/1.3cm seam allowance, sew side and bottom seams. Turn top edge ½"/1.3cm to WS and press. Set aside. Trace one side of strap onto lining fabric. Cut out pieces ½"/1.3cm larger all around. Using a ½"/1.3cm seam allowance, sew one pair of short edges of strap lining tog. Turn all edges ½"/1.3cm to WS and press. Insert bag lining into bag. Slipstitch top edge in place. Fold 2"/5cm St st facings to WS and sew in place. Sew bound-off edges of knitted strap tog. Insert strap lining. Slipstitch short edges to top edge of body lining and long edges to strap.

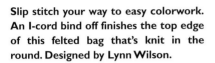

Slip stitch your way to easy colorwork. An I-cord bind off finishes the top edge of this felted bag that's knit in the round. Designed by Lynn Wilson.

KNITTED MEASUREMENTS
Bag

▦ Approx 16"/40.5cm wide x 15"/38cm high x 6"/15cm deep (excluding handles)

Large pocket

▦ Approx 10"/25.5cm wide x 11"/28cm high (after felting)

Small pocket

▦ Approx 5¾"/14.5cm wide x 6½"/16.5cm high (after felting)

MATERIALS

▦ 4 3½oz/100g skeins (each approx 138yd/126m) of Manos del Uruguay/ Design Source *Handspun Semi-Solids* (wool) in #35 uranium (A) **⑤**

▦ 3 skeins in #112 moss multi (B)

▦ Size 11 (8mm) circular needle, 32"/80cm long *or size to obtain gauge*

▦ Two size 11 (8mm) double pointed needles

▦ Stitch marker

▦ One pair 30"/76cm long handles

▦ Matching sewing thread

▦ Sewing needle

▦ 6" x 16"/15 x 40.5cm piece of mat board

▦ ¼yd/.25m lining fabric

▦ ½yd/.5m Lurex sportweight yarn

▦ 4 size 6/0 seed beads

▦ One each size 20mm, 25mm and 30mm clay beads

GAUGE

13 sts to 4"/10cm over St st using size 11 (8mm) needle (before felting).
Take time to check gauge.

Notes

1 Bottom of bag is worked back and forth on circular needle.

2 Body of bag is worked in the round.

3 Each row on chart is work from right to left.

4 Slip all sts purlwise.

5 Carry yarn not in use loosely across WS of all slipped stitches.

SLIP STITCH BODY PATTERN

Rnd 1 *K2, sl 2; rep from *, end k2.
Rnd 2 Knit.
Rnd 3 *Sl 2, k2; rep from *, end sl 2.
Rnd 4 Knit.
Rep rnds 1–4 for sl st body pat.

BAG

Bottom

With B, cast on 59 sts. Work back and forth in garter st for 34 rows. Bind off all sts knitwise.

Body

With RS of bottom facing and B, pick up and k 58 sts along bound-off edge, 16 sts along side edge, 58 sts along cast-on edge and 16 sts along opposite side edge—150 sts. Join and pm for beg of rnds. Purl next rnd. Knit next rnd.

Beg chart pat I

Rnd 1 Work 10-st rep 15 times around. Cont to work chart in this way to rnd 10. With A, cont in sl st body pat for 4½"/11.5cm. Knit next 2 rnds.

Beg chart pat II

Rnd I Work 10-st rep 15 times around. Cont to work chart in this way to rnd 18. With A, cont in sl st body pat for 4½"/11.5cm. Knit next 2 rnds. Work rnds 1–18 of chart pat II once more. With A, cont in sl st body pat for 4½"/11.5cm. Knit next rnd. Change to B and knit next 2 rnds.

I-cord bind-off

Working sts from circular needle to dpn, k4, k2tog tbl—5 sts on dpn. Cont I-cord bind off as foll: **Next row (RS)** *Slide sts to opposite end of dpn, with 2nd dpn, k4, k2tog tbl from circular needle; rep from * around until 5 sts rem on dpn and there are no sts rem on circular needle. Cut yarn leaving a long tail. Join I-cord ends tog.

With B, cast on 40 sts. Work in St st and stripe pat of 4 rows B, 4 rows A until piece measures 17"/43cm from beg, end with a RS row. Knit next 2 rows with B. Bind off loosely.

With B, cast on 22 sts. Work as for large pocket until piece measures 10"/25.5cm from beg, end with a RS row. Knit next 2 rows with B. Bind off loosely.

Felting

Work in all ends before felting. Place pieces into washing machine. Use hot-water wash and a regular (not delicate) cycle. Add ¼ cup of laundry detergent and an old towel or a pair of jeans for extra agitation. Check the pieces periodically to see if they are nice and thick and the knit stitches are no longer visible. Rinse in cold water. Shape bag and pockets to measurements. Dry pieces flat. Position each pocket on WS of bag, so it is 2½"/6.5cm from top edge of bag and centered side to side. Sew in place using sewing thread. Sew on handles 3"/7.5cm down from top edge of bag.

Mat board liner

To cover mat board, cut two 7¼" x 17¼"/18.5 x 44cm pieces from fabric. With RS facing and using a ½"/1.3cm seam allowance, sew around three sides, leaving one short edge open. Turn RS out. Insert mat board. Fold open edge ½"/1.3cm to

WS and whipstitch opening closed. Insert liner into bottom of bag.

Beaded accent

Thread Lurex yarn into tapestry needle. Thread on seed bead, 30mm bead, seed bead, 25mm bead, seed bead, 20mm bead, seed bead. Insert needle back through beads, skipping last seed bead. Even up ends of yarn. Thread both ends into tapestry needle. Sew securely to base of one handle on front as shown in photo.

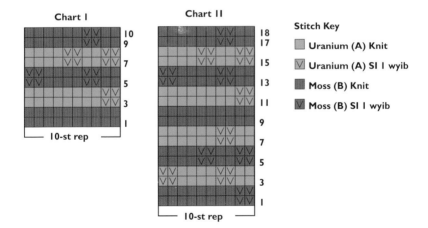

Chart I

10-st rep

Chart II

10-st rep

Stitch Key

■ Uranium (A) Knit

☑ Uranium (A) Sl 1 wyib

■ Moss (B) Knit

☑ Moss (B) Sl 1 wyib

BOX STITCH CLUTCH

Indigo purl

Cleverly crossed and twisted stitches give the appearance of an intricate basket weave. The simplicity of this folded rectangle is a bit deceiving—the basket weave stitch takes time to work. Designed by Cathy Carron.

KNITTED MEASUREMENTS

■ Approx 8"/20.5cm wide x 5½"/14cm high

MATERIALS

■ 1 4oz/113g skein (each approx 121yd/111m) of Cherry Tree Hill *Sachet* (nylon) in tropical storm 〈6〉
■ One pair size 9 (5.5mm) needles *or size to obtain gauge*
■ 1yd/1m of 1½"/38mm wide satin ribbon

GAUGE

19 sts and 20 rows to 4"/10cm over St st using size 9 (5.5mm) needles.
Take time to check gauge.

Note

Bag is made in one piece.

BAG

Cast on 42 sts. Knit 2 rows
Row 1 (RS) *K 2nd st tbl, k first st; rep from * to end.
Row 2 P1, *p 2nd st, p first st; rep from *, end p 1.
Rep these 2 rows until piece measures 13"/33cm from beg, end with a WS row.
Next (bind off) row (RS) K1, *k 2nd st tbl, k first st, pass first 2 sts over last st; rep from *, end k1 and bind off.

FINISHING

Block piece to measurements. Fold cast-on edge up 5½"/13cm, leaving 1½"/4cm free for flap. Sew side seams.

Tie

Thread ribbon around 2 center sts of next to last row of flap. Adjust ribbon so one end is 12"/30.5cm long and remaining end is 24"/61cm long. Tie ribbon once to secure in place. Trim ends at an angle. Wrap longer ribbon end around clutch and tie in a bow.

BOBBLE BAG

Pirate's booty

Chunky bobbles create a fun knitted fabric for this classically shaped handbag. Knit it up using extra-bulky-weight yarn and big needles. Designed by Sima Brason Ferraro.

KNITTED MEASUREMENTS
■ Approx 11"/28cm wide x 7"/18cm high (excluding handle)

MATERIALS
■ 3 3½oz/100g balls (each approx 45yd/41m) of Blue Sky Alpacas *Bulky Hand Dyes* (alpaca/wool) in #1015 orange (6)
■ One pair size 15 (10mm) needles *or size to obtain gauge*
■ Size E/4 (3.5mm) crochet hook
■ One ¾"/2cm magnetic snap
■ ½yd/.5m of medium-weight cotton lining fabric, sewing needle and thread to match
■ One sheet 7 mesh plastic needlepoint canvas
■ 3" x 7"/7.5 x 17.5cm piece of heavy-weight cardboard

GAUGE
3 bobbles to 4½"/11.5cm over bobble pat using size 15 (10mm) needles.
Take time to check gauge.

Note
Sides and bottom of bag are made in one piece.

STITCH GLOSSARY
p2sso Pass the 2 slipped sts over p3tog.

BOBBLE PATTERN
(multiple of 2 plus 1)
Row 1 (RS) Knit.
Row 2 K1, *(p1, yo, p1, yo, p1) in next st (5 sts), k1; rep from * to end.
Row 3 Purl.
Row 4 K1, *sl 2 wyif, p3tog, p2sso, k1; rep from * to end.
Row 5 Knit.
Row 6 K2, *(p1, yo, p1, yo, p1) in next st, k1; rep from *, end k1.
Row 7 Purl.
Row 8 K2, *sl 2 wyif, p3tog, p2sso, k1; rep from *, end k1.
Rep rows 1 to 8 for bobble pat.

BAG
Cast on 17 sts. Work 4 rows in St st for top back facing. Cont in bobble pat for back, rep rows 1–8 3 times (24 rows). Cont in St st for bottom of bag and bind off 1 st at beg of next 2 rows—15 sts. Work even for 8 rows, then cast on 1 st at beg of next 2 rows—17 sts. Cont in bobble pat for front, rep rows 1–8 3 times (24 rows). Cont in St st for 4 rows for top front facing. Bind off.

HANDLE
Cast on 5 sts. Work in St st for 2 rows. Cont in bobble st until piece measures 11½"/29cm from beg, end with a WS row.

Cont in St st for 2 rows. Bind off.

FINISHING

Block pieces to measurements. Sew side seams, then sew bottom edges to side edges of St st section. Fold bag facings to WS and sew in place. Sew on handle, centering each short end on side seam of bag.

Lining

To cover cardboard liner, cut two 4" x 8"/10 x 20.5cm pieces from fabric. With RS facing and using a ½"/1.3cm seam allowance, sew around three sides leaving one short edge open. Turn RS out. Insert cardboard. Fold open edge ½"/1.3cm to WS and whipstitch opening closed. Insert cardboard into bottom of bag. For lining, cut two 12" x 8½"/30.5 x 21.5cm pieces from fabric. With RS facing, sew side and bottom seams using a ½"/1.3cm seam allowance. Square bottom by folding each

corner to a point. Measure 2"/5cm perpendicular to the seam line and mark this line. Sew across marked line. Fold corner points towards bottom and tack in place. Insert lining into bag. Fold top edge of lining to WS, so top edge of lining is ¼"/.6cm from base of bobbles at top edge of bag, then pin-mark for position of each side of magnetic snap. Remove lining. Install snap. Insert lining back into back, then slipstitch top edge of lining in place. For handle liner, cut a 1½" x 12"/4 x 30.5cm strip from plastic canvas. To cover strip, cut two 2½" x 13"/6.5 x 33cm pieces from fabric. Sew pieces tog as for cardboard liner. Turn RS out. Insert canvas strip. Fold open edge ½"/1.3cm to WS and whipstitch opening closed. Slipstitch long edges of handle liner to WS of handle and short edges to top edge of lining.

Gentle waves grace two simple rectangles. Linen yarn and wood handles will have you ready for those summer breezes in no time. Designed by Jenn Jarvis.

KNITTED MEASUREMENTS
▓ Approx 11"/28cm wide x 7"/17.5cm high (excluding handles)

MATERIALS
▓ 2 3½oz/100g balls (each approx 190yd/174m) of Louet Sales *Euroflax Geneva* (linen) in #18.36 natural (4️⃣)
▓ One pair size 5 (3.75mm) needles *or size to obtain gauge*
▓ One pair wooden handles (www.sunbeltfashion.com)
▓ ¼yd/.25m lining fabric, sewing needle and thread to match

GAUGE
24 sts and 28 rows to 4"/10cm over wave pat using size 5 (3.75mm) needles.
Take time to check gauge.

WAVE PATTERN
(multiple of 16 sts plus 3)
Row 1 (RS) K2, *p15, k1; rep from *, end p15, k2.

Row 2 P2, *k15, p1; rep from *, end k15, p2.

Row 3 K2, M1, *p2tog, p11, p2tog, M1, k1, M1; rep from *, end p2tog, p11, p2tog, M1, k2.

Row 4 P3, *k13, p3; rep from *, end k13, p3.

Row 5 K2, M1, k1, M1, *p1, [p2tog] twice, p3, [p2tog] twice, p1, M1, [k1, M1] 3 times; rep from *, end p1, [p2tog] twice, p3, [p2tog] twice, p1,[M1, k1] twice, k1.

Rows 6 and 8 P5, *k9, p7; rep from *, end k9, p5.

Row 7 K5, *p9, k7; rep from *, end p9, k5.

Row 9 K5 *[p2tog] twice, p1, [p2tog] twice, M1, k2, M1, k3, M1, k2, M1; rep from *, end [p2tog] twice, p1, [p2tog] twice, k5.

Row 10 P5, *k5 wrapping yarn around needle twice, p11; rep from *, end k5 wrapping yarn around needle twice, p5.

Row 11 K3, M1, k2, M1, *sl 5 wyib, dropping extra wrap, M1, k4, M1, k3, M1, k4, M1; rep from *, end sl 5 wyib, dropping extra wrap, M1, k2, M1, k3.

Row 12 P7, *p5tog, p15; rep from *, end p5tog, p7.

Row 13 P5, p2tog, *M1, k1, M1, p2tog,

p11, p2tog; rep from *, end M1, k1, M1, p2tog, p5.

Row 14 K6, *p3, k13; rep from *, end p3, k6.

Row 15 P1, [p2tog] twice, p1, *[M1, k1], 3 times, M1, p1, [p2tog] twice, p3, [p2tog] twice, p1; rep from *, end [M1, k1], 3 times, M1, p1, [p2tog] twice, p1.

Rows 16 and 18 K4, *p7, k9; rep from *, end p7, k4.

Row 17 P4, *k7, p9; rep from *, end k7, p4.

Row 19 P4, *M1, k2, M1, k3, M1, k2, M1, [p2tog] twice, p1, [p2tog] twice; rep from *, end M1, k2, M1, k3, M1, k2, M1, p4.

Row 20 K1, k3 wrapping yarn around needle twice, *p11, k5 wrapping yarn around needle twice; rep from *, end p11, k3 wrapping yarn around needle twice, k1.

Row 21 P1, sl 3 wyib, dropping extra wrap, *M1, k4, M1, k3, M1, k4, M1, sl 5 wyib, dropping extra wrap; rep from *, end M1, k4, M1, k3, M1, k4, M1, sl 3 wyib, dropping extra wrap, p1.

Row 22 K1, p3tog, *p15, p5tog; rep from *, end p15, p3tog, k1.

Rep rows 1 to 22 for wave pat.

BACK

Cast on 67 sts. Work in wave pat, rep rows 1 to 22 3 times; piece should measure approx 7"/18cm from beg. Bind off loosely.

FRONT

Work as for back.

FINISHING

Block pieces to measurements. Sew side and bottom seams.

Lining

Cut two 12"/30.5cm x 7"/17.5cm pieces of lining. Using a ½"/1.3cm seam allowance, sew side and bottom seams. Turn top edge ½"/1.3cm to WS and press. Insert lining. Slip stitch top edge of lining to bag. Whipstitch top edge of bag at three points to each handle as shown.

■■■■▭

**Seed stitch gives this sparkly mohair its
nubby texture in this bag designed by
Lynn Wilson. Adorned with wooden
handles and a funky beaded flower, this
bag is one to take everywhere.**

KNITTED MEASUREMENTS
▩ Approx 10"/25.5cm wide x 8"/20cm
high (excluding handles)

MATERIALS
▩ 1 1¾oz/50g ball (each approx
120yd/110m) of Be Sweet *Knobby Ball*
(recycled yarn) in #5a tomato (MC) **⑤**
▩ 1 1¾oz/50g ball (each approx 120yd/
110m) of Be Sweet *Bouclé Mohair*
(mohair) in #5a tomato (A) **⑤**
▩ 1 1¾oz/50g ball (each approx 120yd/
110m) of Be Sweet *Magic Ball* (mohair/
mixed materials) in #mg25 wheatlands
(B) **⑤**
▩ 1 1¾oz/50g ball (each approx 115yd/
105m) of Lion Brand *Glitterspun*
(acrylic/polyester/metallic) in #170 gold
(C) **④**
▩ One pair size 10 (6mm) needles *or
size to obtain gauge*
▩ One pair 5"/12.5cm-diameter round
rattan handles
▩ 12 8 x 6mm faceted acrylic bicone
beads
▩ 40 10/0 rocaille seed beads

▩ Lining fabric, sewing needle and
matching thread

GAUGE
16 sts and 24 rows to 4"/10cm over seed st
using MC and size 10 (6.5mm) needles.
Take time to check gauge.

Note
Bag is made in one piece, beg at back handle edge and ending at front handle edge.

SEED STITCH
Row 1 *K1, p1; rep from * to end.
Row 2 K the purl sts and p the knit sts.
Rep row 2 for seed st.

BAG
With A, loosely cast on 25 sts. Work in
garter st for 2¼"/5.5cm, end with a WS
row. Change to B.
Next (inc) row (RS) K2, inc 1 in next st,
k1, inc 1 in next st, k5, k2tog, k1, k2tog,
k5, inc in next st, k1, inc 1 in next st, k2—
27 sts. Work in seed st for 6 rows.
Next (inc) row (WS) Inc 1 in first st,
work in seed st (as established) to last 2
sts, inc 1 in next st, k1—29 sts. Work in
seed st for 2 rows.
Next (inc) row (RS) Inc 1 in first st, work
in seed st (as established) to last 2 sts, inc
1 in next st, k1—31 sts. Change to MC
and work next row even. Place markers at
beg and end of row. Cont in seed st until
piece measures approx 10"/25.5cm from

markers, end with a RS row. Place markers at beg and end of last row. Change to B.

Next (dec) row (WS) K2tog, work in seed st to last 2 sts, k2tog—29 sts. Work in seed st for 2 rows.

Next (dec) row (RS) K2tog, work in seed st to last 2 sts, k2tog—27 sts. Work in seed st for 6 rows.

Next (dec) row (WS) K2, k2tog, k1, k2tog, k5, inc 1 in next st, k1, inc 1 in next st, k5, k2tog, k1, k2tog, k2—25 sts. Change to A and cont in garter st for 2¼"/5.5cm. Bind off loosely.

FLOWER

With A, cast on 10 sts.

Row 1 (WS) Purl.

Row 2 [K1, p1, k1 in next st] 10 times—30 sts.

Row 3 Purl.

Row 4 [K1, p1, k1 in next st] 30 times—90 sts.

Row 5 Purl. Change to C.

Next (picot bind off) row *Cast on 2 sts, bind off 2 sts, then bind off next 2 sts on LH needle, slip rem st back onto LH needle; rep from *, end work only 1 bind off after last picot.

FINISHING

Block piece to measurements.

Lining

Using bag as a template, cut out fabric lining ½"/1.3cm larger all around than bag. Pin-mark at same points as row markers on bag. With RS tog, fold bag in half and sew side seams to markers; turn RS out. Fold cast-on and bound-off edges over handles and sew in place. With WS tog, fold lining in half and sew side seams to pin markers. Insert lining into bag. Turn all unstitched edges to WS so side edges are even with side edges of bag and top edges butt cast-on and bound-off edges at base of handles. Slip stitch lining in place. Coil flower into shape and sew tog at center to secure. Using needle and thread, sew flower to bag as pictured, stitching through both thicknesses.

Beading

Cut a 36"/91.5cm length of thread. Thread needle and knot one end. Working from WS to RS, insert needle through center of flower. *[Thread on 3 rocaille beads, one bicone] 3 times, thread on 1 rocaille bead, insert needle back through beads skipping last rocaille bead, then insert needle back into bag. Working from WS to RS, insert needle through center of flower; rep from * 3 times more. Secure thread end on WS of bag.

FELTED CLUTCH

Hot cross bag

■■■▢

Colorwork dots and embroidered cross stitches give this clutch the X-Factor. A felted rectangle is folded and topped with a zipper thats accented with a felted pull tab. Designed by Michele Woodford.

KNITTED MEASUREMENTS
▥ Approx 7½"/19cm wide x 4½"/11.5cm wide

MATERIALS
▥ 1 3½oz/100g ball (each approx 223yd/205m) of Patons *Classic Merino Wool* (wool) each in #240 leaf green (A), #230 bright red (B) and #231 chestnut brown (C) **4**
▥ One pair size 7 (4.5mm) needles *or size to obtain gauge*
▥ Zipper 7"/18cm long

GAUGE
20 sts and 26 rows to 4"/10cm over chart pat using size 7 (4.5mm) needles (before felting).
Take time to check gauge.

Notes
1 Bag is made in one piece.
2 When changing colors, twist yarns on WS to prevent holes in work.
3 Carry color not in used loosely on WS of work.
4 Keep all color changes on WS or work.

BAG
With A, cast on 39 sts. Knit 1 row.

Beg chart pat
Row 1 (WS) Beg at st 39 and work to st 1. Cont to work chart in this way to row 48.
Next row (WS) With A, knit. Bind off.

ZIPPER PULL
With B, cast on 6 sts.
Rows 1 and 3 (RS) Sl 1, k 5.
Rows 2 and 4 Sl 1, p5.
Row 5 K2tog, k 2, k2 tog.
Rows 6 and 8 P4.
Row 7 K4.
Row 9 [K2tog] twice.
Row 10 P2. Bind off.

FINISHING
Fold bag in half; sew side seams.

FELTING
Work in all ends before felting. Place pieces in a zippered pillowcase and put into washing machine. Use hot-water wash and a regular (not delicate) cycle. Add ¼ cup of laundry detergent and an old towel or a pair of jeans for extra agitation. Check the pieces periodically to see if they are nice and thick and the knit stitches are barely visible. Rinse in cold water and remove pieces from pillowcase. Shape bag to measurements. Dry pieces flat.

EMBROIDERY
Referring to chart, embroider X's on each side of bag. Baste zipper in place. Sew in zipper. Whipstitch around zipper pull using B, at the same time attaching top to hole in metal zipper pull.

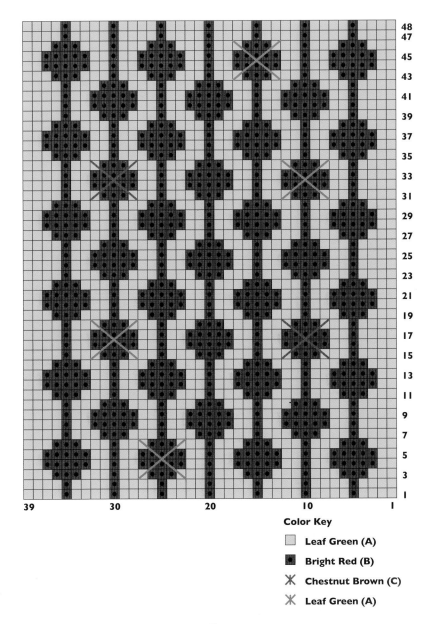

Color Key

☐ Leaf Green (A)

■ Bright Red (B)

✖ Chestnut Brown (C)

✖ Leaf Green (A)

IIIII IIIII IIII IIII

Sumptuous silk yarn and a delicate scallop pattern stitch combine to make one elegant evening bag. You can hold the I-cord doubled to carry as a handbag, or singly to wear as a shoulder bag. Designed by Lisa Hoffman.

KNITTED MEASUREMENTS
■ Approx 10"/25.5cm wide x 8"/20.5cm high (excluding strap)

MATERIALS
■ 2 1¾oz/50g balls (each approx 138yd/126m) of Alchemy Yarns of Transformation *Silk Purse* (silk) in #80a evening pink (⬤3)
■ One pair size 3 (3.25mm) needles *or size to obtain gauge*
■ Two size 3 (3.25mm) double pointed needles
■ Stitch markers
■ Purse frame #SFPH-M06S by Sunbelt Fastener Co. (www.sunbeltfashion.com)
■ ½yd/.5m lining fabric, sewing needle and thread to match

GAUGE
24 sts and 32 rows to 4"/10cm over St st using size 3 (3.25mm) needles.
Take time to check gauge.

Notes
1 Knit the first and last st of every row for selvage sts.
2 The stitch count changes from row to row.

STITCH GLOSSARY
Cluster 5 Sl next 5 sts to dpn and hold to front. Wrap yarn counterclockwise twice around these 5 sts. Place 5 wrapped sts on RH needle.

BACK
Beg at bottom edge, cast on 73 sts.
Row 1 (WS) Knit.
Row 2 K1 (selvedge st), p71, k1 (selvedge st).
Row 3 Knit.
Row 4 K3, pm, k in front and back of next stitch, k21, pm, [yo, k22, pm] twice, k4—76 sts (23 sts between markers).
Row 5 K1, p3, *[p1, k3] twice, p1, k4, [p1, k3] twice, p2, rep; from * to last marker, end p2, k1.
Row 6 K3, *k1, yo, k1, [p3, k1] twice, p4, k1, [p3, k1] twice, yo; rep from * to last marker, end k4—82 sts (25 sts between markers).
Row 7 Keeping 1 st each side in garter st for selvedge sts, work rem sts as they

appear, purling all yo's.

Row 8 K3, *[k1, yo] twice, [ssk, p2] 3 times, [k2tog, p2] twice, k2tog, yo, k1, yo; rep from *, end k4—76 sts (23 sts between markers).

Row 9 Rep row 7.

Row 10 K3, *[k1, yo] 4 times, [ssk, p1] twice, ssk, [k2tog, p1] twice, k2tog, [yo, k1] 3 times, yo; rep from *, end k4—82 sts (25 sts between markers).

Row 11 Rep row 7.

Row 12 K3, *k8, [ssk] twice, k1, M1, k1, [k2tog] twice, k7; rep from *, end k4— to last marker, k4—73 sts (22 sts between markers).

Row 13 Rep row 7.

Row 14 K3, *k9, Cluster 5, k8; rep from *, end k4—73 sts (22 sts between markers). Repeat rows 1–14 twice more, mark beg and end of last row for end of side seam, then rep rows 1–9 once.

Top shaping

Row 10 K3, k across dec 15 sts evenly spaced (dropping markers), end k4—58 sts.

Row 11 K1, p56, p1.

Row 12 K3, k across dec 9 sts evenly spaced, end k4—49 sts.

Row 13 K1, p47, k1.

Row 14 K3, *k5, Cluster 5, k4; rep from *, end k4—49 sts.

Rod pocket

Beg with a purl row, and keeping 1 st each side in garter st for selvedge sts, continue in St st for 4 rows. Knit next row for turning ridge. Beg with a knit row, cont in St st for 4 rows. Bind off.

FRONT

Work as for back.

FINISHING

Do not block.

Lining

Using bag back as a template, cut out two pieces of lining fabric ½"/1.3cm larger than curved edges and top straight edge even with turning ridge of rod pocket. Pin-mark at same points as row markers on bag. With RS tog, sew bottom seam and side seams to markers using a ½"/1.3cm seam allowance; set aside. With RS tog, sew back and front bag tog along bottom seam and side seams to markers; turn RS out. Fold each rod pocket over to WS along turning ridge and hem in place. Unscrew nut from each rod on frame, slip rod through rod pocket, then screw on nut. Wrap side edges of bag over to WS around side edges of frame; sew in place. Insert lining into bag. Turn all unstitched edges to WS so side edges butt side edges of bag and top edges butt bound-off edges at base of rod pockets. Slip stitch lining in place.

I-cord handles

With dpn, cast on 4 sts. Work I-cord over these 4 sts as foll: ***Next row (RS)** With 2nd dpn, k4, do not turn. Slide sts back to beg of needle to work next row from RS; rep from * until I-cord measures 24"/ 61cm. Bind off, leaving a long tail for sewing. Thread I-cord through handle eyelets, then sew ends of I-cord tog.

WOVEN MESSENGER BAG
American I-cord

This bag is worked in stockinette stitch with **reverse stockinette stitch side gussets.The woven design is added later for a quick project. Designed by Jutta Zuloaga.**

KNITTED MEASUREMENTS

■ Approx 15"/38cm wide x 10"/25.5cm high x 1¾"/4.5cm deep (excluding strap)

MATERIALS

■ 6 2oz/56g balls (each approx 70yd/ 64m) of La Lana Wools *Forever Random Handspun* (wool/mohair) in #te morada (MC) (4)

■ 3 4oz/112g balls (each approx 200yd/ 183m) of La Lana Wools *Millspun wool* (wool) in #kota (A) (4)

■ 1 ball in #logwood purple (B)

■ One pair each size 10 and 11 (6 and 8mm) needles *or size to obtain gauge*

■ Size J/10 (6mm) crochet hook

■ Stitch holder

■ One ⅞"/22mm button

■ Two 8"/20.5cm and four 14"/35.5cm lengths of ½"/13mm diameter wooden dowels

■ 3yd/3m of ½"/13mm diameter cable cord

GAUGE

14 sts and 20 rows to 4"/10cm over St st using MC and larger needles.
Take time to check gauge.

PIPING

Piping Row (RS) Fold piece up, WS tog, *pick up 1 st in the back of st 10 rows below and knit it tog with next st on LH needle; rep from * to end.

BAG

Front flap

With smaller needles and B, cast on 48 sts. Work in St st for 10 rows. Change to A and work piping row. Beg with a p row, cont in St st for 35 rows. Change to B and work in St st for 10 rows. Change to MC and work piping row.

Top gusset

Beg with a p row, cont in St st for 9 rows.

Back of bag

Change to B and work in St st for 10 rows. Change to MC and work piping row. Beg with a p row, cont in St st for 49 rows. Change to B and work in St st for 10 rows. Change to MC and work piping row.

Bottom gusset

Beg with a p row, cont in St st for 9 rows.

Front of bag

Change to B and work in St st for 10 rows. Change to MC and work piping row. Beg with a p row, cont in St st for 49 rows. Change to B and work in St st for 10 rows, then work piping row. Bind off.

WOVEN COVER

Warp (vertical strips)
(make 18)
With smaller needles and MC, cast on 4 sts. Work in St st for 36 rows. Bind off. Make 8 more using MC, 5 using A and 4 using B.

Weft (horizontal strips)
(make 9)
With smaller needles and MC, cast on 4 sts. Work in St st for 50 rows. Bind off. Make 4 more using MC, 2 using A and 2 using B.

Side piping
(make 2)
With larger needles and B, cast on 8 sts. Work in St st for 36 rows. Bind off.

SIDE GUSSETS/STRAP

With larger needles and MC, pick up and k 7 sts along side edge of bottom gusset. Beg with a k row, cont in rev St st for 49 rows, place sts on holder for first side gusset. Work 2nd side gusset as for first until 49 rows have been completed. Change to A and work even in St st for 32"/81cm, end with a WS row. Weave strap sts and first side gusset sts tog using Kitchener st.

Gusset/strap piping
(make 2)
With larger needles and A, cast on 8 sts. Work in St st for 52"/132cm. Bind off.

FINISHING

Sew ends of warp strips to front flap, placing them in order as foll: *MC, A, MC, B; rep from * across. Working from top to bottom, weave weft strips over and under warp strips, sewing ends in place to front flap and placing them in order as foll: *MC, A, MC, B; rep from * down. Sew each side piping strip to side of front flap to conceal ends of weft strips. Fold piping over to WS and sew in place. With crochet hook and A, sc side gussets to sides of bag. Beg at bottom edge of bag, sew one side edge of gusset/strap piping up edge of first side gusset, along strap, then down opposite side gusset. Cut cable cord in half. Place cord inside piping, trim off excess if necessary, then sew opposite edge of piping closed. Rep for rem gusset/strap piping. Insert a longer dowel into each horizontal piping. Insert each shorter dowel into each vertical piping. Sew adjacent edges of piping tog to close. With crochet hook and A, ch 3"/7.5cm for button loop. Sew to WS of flap. Sew button to lower edge of front, opposite button loop.

◼◼◼◼▶

Felted, colorful entralac squares make this bag a must-have. Stockinette stitch straps are made separately and sewn on before felting. Designed by Cecelia Madison.

KNITTED MEASUREMENTS
◼ Approx 10½"/26.5 wide x 9¼"/23.5 high (excluding straps)

MATERIALS
◼ 2 3½oz/100g balls (each approx 220yd/201m) of Nashua Handknits/ Westminster Fibers, Inc. *Creative Focus Worsted* (wool/alpaca) in #500 ebony (MC) (**4**)
◼ 1 ball each in #401 nickel (A), #202 camel (B), #2380 oatmeal (C), #3249 chocolate (D), #100 natural (E), #1650 jeans (F), and #4899 khaki green (G)
◼ Size 9 (5.5mm) circular needle, 32"/80cm long *or size to obtain gauge*
◼ Two size 9 (5.5mm) double pointed needles
◼ Stitch marker

GAUGE
One square to 2½"/6.5cm using size 9 (5.5mm) needles (before felting).
Take time to check gauge.

BAG

Square 1

With MC, cast on 10 sts. K 20 rows, do not cut yarn.

Square 2

*With same MC, cast on 10 sts using cable cast-on. K 20 rows, do not cut yarn; rep from * twice more for squares 3 and 4—40 sts on needle.

Square 5

Sl 10 sts of square 4 to RH needle. With E, pick up and k 10 sts along left side of square 4. *Turn and k10, turn, k9, k last st tog with first st of square 3; rep from * until no sts of square 3 rem. Cut yarn.

Square 6

With A, pick up and k 10 sts along left side of square 3. *Turn and k10, turn, k9, k last st tog with first st of square 3; rep from * until no sts of square 3 rem. Cut yarn.

Square 7

With E, pick up and k 10 sts along left side of square 2. *Turn and k10, turn, k9, k last st tog with first st of square 1; rep from * until no sts of square 1 rem. Cut yarn.

Square 8

Turn piece so that square 1 is on the right and square 4 is on the left. With a spare needle, pick up and k 10 sts from the cast-on row of square 2. With E, pick up and k 10 sts along right side of square 1. *Turn and k10, turn, k9, k last st tog with first st of square 2; rep from * until no sts of square 2 rem. Cut yarn.

Square 9

With a spare needle, pick up and k 10 sts from the cast-on row of square 3. With A, pick up and k 10 sts along right side of square 2. *Turn and k10, turn, k9, k last st tog with first st of square 3; rep from * until no sts of square 3 rem. Cut yarn.

Square 10

With a spare needle, pick up and k 10 sts from the cast-on row of square 4. With E, pick up and k 10 sts along right side of square 3. *Turn and k10, turn, k9, k last st tog with first st of square 4; rep from * until no sts of square 4 rem. Cut yarn.

Note Squares 11, 14, 15 and 18 are picked up from the sides of squares 1 and 4 in order to form the corners at the base of the bag. Your work will no longer lie flat after these squares are worked.

Square 11

With B, pick up and k 10 sts from the right side of square 4. *Turn and k10, turn, k9, k last st tog with first st of square 10; rep from * until no sts of square 10 rem. Cut yarn.

Square 12

Sl 10 sts of square 11 to LH needle. With D, pick up and k 10 sts from the right side of square 10. *Turn and k10, turn, k first

st tog with last st of square 9; rep from * until no sts of square 9 rem. Cut yarn.

Square 13

Sl 10 sts of square 12 to LH needle. With D, pick up and k 10 sts from the right side of square 9. *Turn and k10, turn, k first st tog with last st of square 8; rep from * until no sts of square 8 rem. Cut yarn.

Square 14

Sl 10 sts of square 13 to LH needle. With spare needle, pick up and 10 sts from the cast on row of square 1. With C, pick up and k 10 sts from the right side of square 8. *Turn and k10, turn, k first st tog with last st of square 1; rep from * until no sts of square 1 rem. Cut yarn.

Cont as established, referring to placement diagram for color and direction of each square worked.

Top triangles

With MC, pick up and k 10 sts from left side of square 50. *Turn, k10, turn, k9, k last st tog with first st of square 49; rep from * until no sts of square 49 rem. Sl the 1 rem st to RH needle and bind it off over the first st picked up for the next triangle. Work 7 more triangles around top of bag. Bind off final st.

BAND

With RS facing and MC, pick up and k 10 sts across each triangle—80 sts. Pm for beg of rnd. Work in rnds of garter st (p 1 rnd, k 1 rnd) for 9 rnds. Bind off purlwise.

STRAPS

(make 2)
With MC, cast on 120 sts. K 8 rows. Bind off purlwise.

FINISHING

Sew straps to bag (below band) at each point of side diamond.

Felting

Work in all ends before felting. Place piece in a zippered pillowcase and put into washing machine. Use hot-water wash and a regular (not delicate) cycle. Add a tablespoon of laundry detergent and let the pieces agitate. Check the pieces frequently, agitating until desired felting is achieved; do no overfelt. Rinse in cold water and remove piece from pillowcase. Shape bag to finished measurements, then allow to air dry.

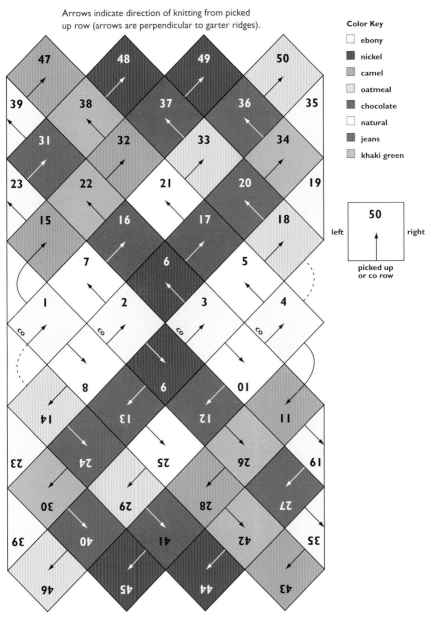

Arrows indicate direction of knitting from picked up row (arrows are perpendicular to garter ridges).

Color Key

- ☐ ebony
- ■ nickel
- ■ camel
- ☐ oatmeal
- ■ chocolate
- ☐ natural
- ■ jeans
- ■ khaki green

left [50 ↑] right

picked up or co row

■■■▭

Update an old-fashioned argyle pattern with knit-in shell buttons. This hobo-style shoulder bag is fun to knit in the round using glittery wool yarn. Tie the top closed with I-cord ties. Designed by Michele Woodford.

KNITTED MEASUREMENTS
▥ Approx 11"/28cm wide x 8½"/21.5cm high x 2"/5cm deep (excluding strap)

MATERIALS
▥ 4 1¾oz/50g balls (each approx 105yd/96m) of Skacel Collection *Gentry* (wool/nylon/metallic) in #6 silver 🎨
▥ Size 7 (4.5mm) circular needle, 16"/40cm long *or size to obtain gauge*
▥ Two each sizes 6 and 7 (4 and 4.5mm) double pointed needles
▥ Size 7 (1.65mm) steel crochet hook
▥ Stitch holders and markers.
▥ 130 ¾"/19mm shell buttons with a single hole or 20mm paillettes
▥ 2yd/2m ⅝"/16mm wide satin ribbon
▥ Sewing needle and matching thread

GAUGE
18 sts and 24 rnds to 4"/10cm over St st using size 7 (4.5mm) needle.
Take time to check gauge.

Notes
I Each half of bottom of bag is worked back and forth on circular needle.

2 Body of bag is worked in the round.
3 Each row on chart is work from right to left.
4 To add a shell button or paillette, insert crochet hook into hole of button (or paillette). Use hook to remove st from LH needle, then draw this st through hole. Use hook to place st back on LH needle, then knit the st in the usual manner.

BAG
Bottom
With circular needle, cast on 39 sts. Work back and forth in garter st for 10 rows; place sts on holder. With circular needle, cast on another 39 sts. Work back and forth in garter st for 10 rows.
Next rnd K 39 sts from holder, cast on 9 sts, k next 39 sts on needle, then cast on 9 sts—96 sts. Pm for beg rnds.
Body
Beg with a p rnd, work around in garter st for 8 rnds. Knit next 2 rnds.
Beg chart pat
Rnd I Work 12-st rep 6 times adding shell buttons (or paillettes) as described in note. Cont in this manner through rnd 39. Knit next rnd.
Divide for strap
Next rnd K33, k15 and place sts on holder for strap, k33, k15 and place sts on holder for strap.

Top edging

Next 2 rows *P33 turn, wyif, sl next st, turn; rep from * once more. Bind off sts knitwise. Rep for other side of bag.

First half of strap

Slip 15 sts from holder to smaller dpn. Purl next row.

Next (dec) row (RS) K 1, ssk, k to last 3 sts, k2tog, k1. Work next 3 rows even. Rep last 4 rows 3 times more—7 sts. Change to larger dpn and work I-cord over these 7 sts as foll: ***Next row (RS)** With 2nd dpn, k7, do not turn. Slide sts back to beg of needle to work next row from RS; rep from * until I-cord measures 16"/ 40.5cm. Place sts on holder.

Second half of strap

Work as for first half. Weave sts tog using Kitchener st.

FINISHING

Sew center and corner seams on bottom of bag. Thread ribbon through I-cord strap. Making sure ribbon is centered side to side, turn cut ends of ribbon to WS and sew in place. Sew side edges of ribbon to WS of strap to beg of I-cord rows.

I-cord ties (make 2)

With smaller dpn, cast on 3 sts. Work I-cord over these 3 sts as foll: ***Next row (RS)** With 2nd dpn, k3, do not turn. Slide sts back to beg of needle to work next row from RS; rep from * until I-cord measures 12"/30.5cm. Cut yarn leaving a long tail.

Thread tail in tapestry needle and weave through sts. Pull tight to gather, fasten securely, then sew a shell button (or paillette) to end of I-cord. Sew other end to center top edge of bag.

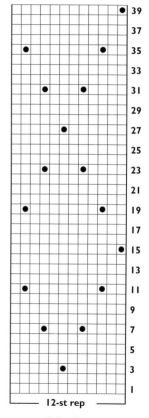

12-st rep

Color Key

☐ Knit

◉ Add Shell button (or paillette)

Send them off to school in cheery style with this brightly colored backpack. Just fold the double seed stitch rectangle in half and sew side seams. Add straps and a drawstring closure and they're ready to go. Designed by Mary Bonnette.

KNITTED MEASUREMENTS

■ Approx 9½"/24cm wide x 11½"/29cm high (excluding straps)

MATERIALS

■ 3 1¾oz/50g skeins (each approx 108yd/99m) of Tahki Yarns/Tahki•Stacy Charles, Inc., *Cotton Classic* (mercerized cotton) in #3723 lime (MC) (4)

■ 1 skein each in #3450 fuchsia (A), #3002 black (B) and #3001 white (C)

■ One pair size 8 (5mm) needles *or size to obtain gauge*

■ Size H/8 (5mm) crochet hook

GAUGE

16 sts and 26 rows to 4"/10cm over double seed st using 2 strands of yarn and size 8 (5mm) needles.
Take time to check gauge.

Notes

1 Use 2 strands of yarn held tog throughout.

2 Bag is made in one piece, beg at back top edge and ending at front top edge.

DOUBLE SEED STITCH
(multiple of 4 sts)
Rows 1 and 2 *K2, p2; rep from * to end.
Rows 3 and 4 *P2, k2; rep from * to end.
Rep rows 1 to 4 for double seed st.

BAG

With 2 strands of A held tog, cast on 48 sts. Work in double seed st for 6 rows. Change to 2 strands of B. Purl next row.
Next row (RS) *K2 C, k2 B; rep from * to end.
Next row *P2 B, p2 C; rep from * to end.
With B, knit next row.
Change to 2 strands of MC and purl next row. Cont in double seed st until piece measures 18"/45.5cm from beg, end with a WS row. With MC, knit next row.
Change to 2 strands of B, purl next row.
Next row (RS) *K2 C, k2 B; rep from * to end.
Next row *P2 B, p2 C; rep from * to end.
With B, knit next row.
Change to 2 strands of A, purl next row.
Cont in double seed st for 6 rows. Bind off.

FINISHING

Block piece to measurements. Fold piece in half, then sew side seams.

Straps

(make 2)

With crochet hook and 2 strands of B, make a ch 20"/51cm long. Fasten off. Sew one end to side seam, 1½"/4cm from top edge. Sew opposite end to back of bag, ½"/1.3cm from side seam and ½"/1.3cm from bottom fold.

Drawstring

With crochet hook, 2 strands of A and leaving a long tail, make a ch 30"/76cm long. Fasten off leaving a long tail. Beg at center front, weave drawstring through B/C stripe at top edge of bag.

Tassels

(make 2)

Cut six strands of A, 7"/18cm long. Use crochet hook to draw ends of strands through one end of drawstring; even up strand ends. Wrap drawstring tail 3 times around tassel to secure strands, then fasten off tail securely.

Bring home the goodies in this generously sized, eyelet patterned bag. Wide garter stitch handles make it easy to carry and drawstring closure keeps the contents secure. Knit it using a double strand of pretty, yet very sturdy linen yarn. Designed by Michele Woodford.

KNITTED MEASUREMENTS

- Approx 18"/46cm wide x 14"/35.5cm high (excluding handles)

MATERIALS

- 2 3½oz/100g balls (each approx 190yd/ 174m) of Louet Sales *Euroflax Geneva* (linen) in #18.01 champagne (MC) **(4)**
- 1 ball in #18.47 terra cotta (CC)
- Size 11 (8mm) circular needle, 24"/60cm long or size to obtain gauge
- One pair size 9 (5.5mm) needles
- Size I/9 (5.5mm) crochet hook
- Stitch marker
- Four large wooden beads (optional)

GAUGE

12 sts and 14 rnds to 4"/10cm over St st using using 2 strands of yarn and larger needle.

Take time to check gauge.

Notes

1 Use 2 strands of yarn held tog throughout.
2 Bag is made in one piece
3 Each handle/strap is made separately.

EYELET PATTERN

(multiple of 6 sts)

Rnd 1 K1, *k2tog, yo twice, ssk, k2; rep from *, end last rep k1.

Rnd 2 K2, *work (k1, p1 in double yo), k4; rep from *, end last rep k2.

Rnd 3 Yo, ssk, *k2, k2tog, yo twice, ssk; rep from *, end last rep k2tog, yo.

Rnd 4 P1 in yo, k4, *work (k1, p1 in double yo), k4; rep from *, end last rep k1 in yo.

Rep rnds 1–4 for eyelet pat.

BAG

With circular needle and 1 strand MC and CC held tog, cast on 90 sts. Join, taking care not to twist sts on needle. Pm for beg of rnd. Work around in garter st for 22 rnds. Knit next rnd. Cont in eyelet pat, rep rows 1–4 3 times.

Change to 2 strands of MC. Cont in eyelet pat, rep rows 1–4 3 times.

Change to 2 strands of CC. Cont in eyelet pat, rep rows 1–4 twice.

HANDLE/STRAP

(make 2)

With smaller needles and 2 strands of MC held tog, cast on 4 sts. Work in garter st for 48"/122cm. Bind off.

FINISHING

Block pieces to measurements. Sew bottom edges of bag tog. Sew short edges of each handle/strap tog. Place bag flat on work surface. Position first handle/strap around bag, matching seams and so outer side edge of handle/strap is 3"/8cm from side edge of bag. Pin in place beg at bottom edge to beg of CC eyelet rnds. Using one strand of CC, whipstitch side edges of handle/strap in place. Rep for rem handle/strap.

Drawstring

With crochet hook and 1 strand of MC and CC held tog, ch 48"/122cm. Beg and ending at center front, weave drawstring through eyelets of next to last row. Thread beads onto drawstring ends, then knit ends to secure.

FELTED TOTE

Felt like watermelon

Simple stripes worked in colorful wool yarn make this an around-town kind of bag. Felting gives it durability for everyday use. Designed by Lisa Valentino.

KNITTED MEASUREMENTS

■ Approx 8½"/21.5 wide x 9"/23cm high (excluding handles)

MATERIALS

■ 1 4oz/113g ball (each approx 190yd/ 174m) of Brown Sheep Company *Lamb's Pride Worsted* (wool/mohair) each in #M68 pine tree (A), #M120 limeade (B) and #M38 lotus pink (C) (4)

■ One set (5) size 10½ (6.5mm) double pointed needles *or size to obtain gauge*

■ Stitch holders and markers

GAUGE

16 sts and 20 rnds to 4"/10cm over St st using size 10½ (6.5mm) dpns (before felting).

Take time to check gauge.

Note

Bag is worked in the round from the bottom up.

BAG

With A, cast on 9 sts. Divide sts evenly between 3 needles with 3 sts on each needle. Join, taking care not to twist sts on needle. Pm for beg of rnd and sl marker every rnd. K next rnd.

Next (inc) rnd *K1, inc 1 in next st; rep from *, end k1—13 sts. K next rnd.

Next (inc) rnd *Inc 1 in each st around— 26 sts. K next 2 rnds.

Next (inc) rnd *K1, inc 1 in next st; rep from * around—39 sts. K next 3 rnds.

Next (inc) rnd *K2, inc 1 in next st; rep from * around—52 sts. K next 4 rnds.

Next (inc) rnd *K2, inc 1 in next st; rep from *, end k1—69 sts. K next 4 rnds.

Next (inc) rnd *K2, inc 1 in next st; rep from * around—92 sts. K next 5 rnds.

Next (dec) rnd *K13, k2tog; rep from *, end k2—86 sts. K next 15 rnds.

Beg stripe pat

Change to B and k next 3 rnds. Change to C and k next 45 rnds. Change to B and k next 2 rnds.

Next rnd [K5 sts, place on holder for strap, bind off 25 sts, k5 place on holder for strap, bind off 8 sts] twice.

HANDLE

With RS facing and B, sl 5 sts from a st holder to dpn. Work in I-cord as foll: ***Next row (RS)** With 2nd dpn, k5, do not turn. Slide sts back to beg of needle to work next row from RS; rep from * until I-cord measures 12"/30.5cm. Cut yarn. Join I-cord to 5 sts on holder on same side of bag using Kitchener stitch or 3-needle bind-off. Rep for opposite side of bag for second handle.

FINISHING

Felting

Place piece in a zippered pillowcase and put into washing machine. Use hot-water wash and a regular (not delicate) cycle. Add a tablespoon of laundry detergent and an old pair of jeans for agitation. Check the piece frequently, agitating until stitches are not seen. Rinse in cold water and remove piece from pillowcase. Shape bag to finished measurements, then allow to air dry. Shape bag by placing a 4–5"/10–12.5cm diameter plate, lid, or bowl in bottom of bag and stretching gently into shape. Allow to dry completely.

FELTED SHOULDER BAG
Green giant

Oversized, relaxed and easy-to-wear, this trendy felted shoulder bag is accented with beaded flaps on front and back. Knit it in stockinette stitch working short rows to give the bag its appealing banana shape. Designed by Heather Brack.

KNITTED MEASUREMENTS

■ Approx 20"/51cm wide x 9"/23cm high (excluding strap)

MATERIALS

■ 6 1¾oz/50g balls (each approx 87yd/80m) of Frog Tree Yarns *Alpaca Worsted* (alpaca) in #41 green (**3**)
■ One pair size 10½ (6.5mm) needles *or size to obtain gauge*
■ Size 2 (2.25mm) steel crochet hook
■ Stitch markers
■ 36 glass pony beads
■ One ¾"/2cm magnetic snap

GAUGE

16 sts to 4"/10cm over St st using size 10½ (6.5mm) needles (before felting).
Take time to check gauge.

Note
To add a pony bead, insert crochet hook into hole. Use hook to remove sl st from LH needle, then draw this st through hole. Use hook to place st back on LH needle, then purl the st in the usual manner.

STITCH GLOSSARY

w & t (wrap and turn) Work to turning point. Sl next st to RH needle. Bring yarn to front between needles and sl st back to LH needle.

BACK

Beg at end of strap, cast on 1 st.
Next row (RS) Inc 1 (k into front and back of st)—2 sts. Purl next row.
Next (inc) row Inc 1, k1—3 sts. Purl next row.
Next (inc) row [Inc 1 twice], k1—5 sts. Purl next row.
Next (inc) row Inc 1, k to last 2 sts, inc 1, k1—7 sts. Purl next row.
Rep last 2 rows 3 times more—13 sts. Cont in St st until piece measures 8"/20.5cm from beg, end with a WS row.
Next row (RS) K5, M1, k1, pm, k1, pm, k1, M1, k5—15 sts. Work 3 rows even.
Next (inc) row K to 1 st before marker, M1, k to 2nd marker, k1, M1, k to end—17 sts. Work 3 rows even. Rep last 4 rows 12 times more—41 sts.
Next (inc) row K to 1 st before marker, M1, k to 2nd marker, k1, M1, k to end—43 sts. Purl next row. Rep last 2 rows 14 times more—71 sts.

Beg short rows
Next row (RS) Knit to last 2 sts (working incs as established), w & t.
Next row Purl to last 2 sts, w & t. Rep

these 2 rows 4 times more. Cont short rows and incs outside the markers and work incs inside the markers as foll:

Row 1 Inc 1.

Row 2 Purl.

Row 3 [K1, M1] twice, k1.

Row 4 Purl.

Row 5 K1, M1, k3, M1, k1.

Row 6 Purl.

Row 7 K1, M1, k5, M1, k1. Cont as established until there are 13 sts between markers. Purl next row.

Next row (RS) Knit, working the wrap st and the knit st tog.

Next row Purl, working the wrap st and the purl st tog. There should be 47 sts before first marker, 15 sts between markers, and 47 sts after markers.

Row 1 (RS) K16, p1, k to 2nd marker, k30, p1, k to end.

Row 2 K the knit sts and p the purl sts.

Row 3 K16, p2, k to 2nd marker, k29, p2, k to end.

Rows 4 to 6 Rep row 2.

Row 7 K16, p3, k10, p1, k to 2nd marker, k17, p1, k10, p3, k to end.

Row 8 Rep row 2.

Row 9 K16, p3, k9, p2, k to 2nd marker, k17, p2, k9, p3, k to end.

Rows 10 to 14 Rep row 2.

Row 15 K10, p1, k5, p4, k8, p2, k to 2nd marker, k17, p2, k8, p4, k5, p1, k to end.

Row 16 Rep row 2.

Row 17 K10, p1, k5, p4, k5, p1, k2, p2, k to 2nd marker, k17, p2, k2, p1, k5, p4, k5, p1, k to end.

Row 18 Rep row 2.

Row 19 K9, p2, k5, p4, k4, p2, k2, p3, k to 2nd marker, k16, p3, k2, p2, k4, p4, k5, p2, k to end.

Rows 20 to 26 Rep row 2. Bind off.

FRONT

Work as for back.

BEADED FLAP

(make 2)

Cast on 11 sts.

Rows 1, 3 and 5 Purl.

Rows 2 and 4 Knit.

Row 6 K2, [sl 1, k1] 3 times, sl 1, k2.

Row 7 Purl across, adding pony beads to each sl st as described in note.

Row 8 Knit.

Row 9 Purl.

Row 10 K3, [sl 1, k1] twice, sl 1, k3.

Row 11 Rep row 7.

Row 12 Knit.

Row 13 Purl. Rep rows 6–13 once more, then rows 6–9 once.

Row 26 Knit.

Row 27 Purl.

Row 28 Knit. Bind off.

FINISHING

Sew bound-off edges of back and front tog. On front, position a beaded flap over seam and so top edge of flap is even with top edge of bag. Sew top and bottom edges of flap in place. Sew rem beaded flap to back of bag.

Felting

Work in all ends before felting. Place piece in a zippered pillowcase and put into washing machine. Use hot-water wash and a regular (not delicate) cycle. Add ¼ cup of laundry detergent and an old towel or a pair of jeans for extra agitation. Check the piece periodically to see if the fabric is nice and thick and the knit stitches are barely visible. Rinse in cold water and remove piece from pillowcase. Shape bag to measurements. Dry flat. On underside of strap, bring edges so they meet. Beg 2"/5cm from top edge of bag, sew edges tog for 1"/2.5cm. Rep for other strap. Install magnetic snap under beaded flaps. Knot strap ends tog.

This beautiful bag, designed by Margery Winter, is not only fun to make, but a kick to decorate with an array of fabulous accents. Start with weaving a fun contrasting fringe through the slip stitches on the bag and the garter stitches on the handle. Next, make a bouquet of funky flowers and sew on in a carefree arrangement. Finish with a chunky twisted cord drawstring to tie the top closed.

KNITTED MEASUREMENTS

■ Approx 15"/40.5cm wide x 8"/20.5cm high (excluding handle)

MATERIALS

■ 3 1¾oz/50g balls (each approx 120yd/111m) of Berroco, Inc. *Suede* (nylon) in #3715 tonto (MC) **④**

■ 1 ball each in #3745 calamity jane (A) and #3718 holster (B)

■ 1 1¾oz/50g ball (each approx 120yd/111m) of Berroco, Inc. *Suede Tri-Color* (nylon) each in #3795 cisco kid (C) and #3793 buffalo bill (D) **④**

■ One pair size 8 (5mm) needles *or size to obtain gauge*

■ Size 8 (5mm) circular needle, 24"/60cm long

■ Two 1"/25mm hinged metal purse rings

GAUGE

21 sts and 32 rows to 4"/10cm over slip st pat using size 8 (5mm) needles.
Take time to check gauge.

Note

Body of bag is made vertically in one piece from side seam to side seam.

SLIP STITCH PATTERN

(multiple of 3 sts plus 2)
Row 1 (RS) Knit.
Rows 2 and 3 Knit.
Rows 4 and 6 *K2, sl 1 wyif; rep from *, end k2.
Row 5 *K2, sl 1 wyib; rep from *, end k2.
Rows 7 and 8 Knit.
Rep rows 1 to 8 for slip st pat.

BAG

With MC, cast on 77 sts. Work in slip st pat until piece measures approx 16"/40.5cm from beg, end with row 8. Bind off. Fold piece in half, RS facing and sew cast-of edge tog, then sew bound-off edge tog.

Top border

With RS facing, circular needle, MC, and beg at any side seam, pick up and k 44 sts to opposite side seam, then 44 sts to beg side seam—88 sts. Pm for beg of rnds. Purl next rnd.

Next (eyelet) rnd *K2, yo, SKP; rep from * around. Purl next 2 rnds. Change to

A. Knit next rnd. Purl next rnd. Bind off.

HANDLE

With 2 strands of MC held tog, cast on 6 sts. Work in garter st until piece measures 14"/35.5cm from beg. Bind off.

SMALL FLOWER

(make 10)

With C, cast on 6 sts leaving a long tail for sewing.

Next (inc) row (RS) [K into front and back of next st] 6 times—12 sts. Purl next row.

Next (inc) row (RS) [K into front and back of next st] 12 times—24 sts. Purl next row.

Next (inc) row (RS) [K into front and back of next st] 24 times—48 sts. Purl next row. Bind off leaving a long tail for sewing. Make 4 more using C and 5 more using D.

LARGE FLOWER

(make 10)

With C, work as for small flower until 6 rows have been completed—48 sts.

Next (inc) row (RS) [K into front and back of next st] 48 times—96 sts. Purl next row. Bind off leaving a long tail for sewing. Make 4 more using C and 5 more using D.

FINISHING

Bag stripes

Cut 3 strands of A, 26"/66cm long. Beg at first vertical row of slip sts at right side seam. Leaving 6"/15cm at each end, weave strands down through slip sts on front of bag, then up through slip sts on back of bag. On front and back of bag, knot strands close to last slip st, then weave strands under next slip st and knot ends again to secure in place. Knot strands 1"/2.5cm from last knot, then knot close to ends. Working from right to left, cont to weave strands alternating B and A. Open hinged ring and thread through four eyelets at right side of bag. Rep on left side of bag with rem ring. Whipstitch handle to purse rings using MC.

Handle stripes

Cut 2 strands of A, 34"/86.5cm long. Beg at right side edge. Leaving 10"/25.5cm at each end, weave strands through garter sts on front of handle. Working from right to left, cont to weave 2 strands each B, C, B and A. Gather strands tog and knot three times to form one big knot. Trim ends close to last knot.

Handle wraps

Cut two strands of B 50"/127cm long; thread into tapestry needle. Working 3"/7.5cm from end of handle, wrap yarn

14 times around handle, covering 1"/2.5cm of handle. On right side of handle, wrap yarn 4 times around wraps, pulling tight to gather in strands; fasten off securely on WS of handle.

Flowers

Roll cast-on edge of each flower to form flower shape, then sew securely with a tail. Refer to photo. Use rem tail to sew flowers to front sides and bottom edge of bag, arranging sizes and colors as shown or desired.

Drawstring

Cut 4 strands of A 60"/152.5cm long. Fold strands in half, then knot cut ends tog. Attach knot to a fixed object. Insert a pencil into fold end. Turn pencil counter clockwise until strands are twisted tightly tog. Pull strands straight, fold in half, holding fold firmly in your right hand, then hold knotted end with pencil firmly in your left hand. Release the folded strands from your right hand, allowing all strands to twist tog. Tie each end into a knot, knotting beyond the previous knot. Trim ends to neaten. Weave drawstring through eyelets around top edge of bag, beg and ending at center front. Knot each end of drawstring twice more to form one big knot.

EYE POD PURSE

Purl vision

This felted "eye" pod is a must for those on the go. Designed by Mags Kandis.

KNITTED MEASUREMENTS

Approx 6"/15cm wide x 9"/23cm high (excluding strap)

MATERIALS

■ 1 3½oz/100g ball (each approx 223yd/205m) of Patons *Classic Merino Wool* (wool) each in #208 burgundy (MC), #240 leaf green (A), #77134 that's blue (B) and #204 old gold (C) 🏷

■ One pair size 10½ (6.5mm) needles *or size to obtain gauge*

■ Size J/10 (6mm) crochet hook

■ One ⅝"/16mm button

GAUGE

15 sts and 21 rows to 4"/10cm over St st using size 10½ (6.5mm) needles (before felting).

Take time to check gauge.

Note

Bag is made in one piece, beg at flap and ending at bottom edge of bag.

BAG

Beg at botton edge of flap, with MC, cast on 31 sts. Work in St st for 36 rows.

Next Row (RS) K1, M1, k30, cast on 31 sts for body of bag using backward loop method—62 sts. Beg with a p row, work in St st for 61 rows.

Bottom shaping

Row I (RS) K1, [k8, k2tog] 6 times, k1—56 sts.

Row 2 and all WS rows Purl.

Row 3 K1, [k7, k2tog] 6 times, k1—50 sts.

Row 5 K1, [k6, k2tog] 6 times, k1—44 sts.

Row 7 K1, [k5, k2tog] 6 times, k1—38 sts. Cont to dec in this manner, working 1 less st before the dec, every RS row until 14 sts rem, end with a WS row.

Next row (RS) K1, [k2tog] 6 times, k1—8 sts. Cut yarn leaving a long tail. Thread tail in tapestry needle and weave through rem sts. Pull tight to gather, fasten off securely, then sew side seam.

APPLIQUÉS

Square I

With A, cast on 26 sts. Work in St st for 32 rows. Bind off.

Square 2

With B, cast on 18 sts. Work in St st for 20 rows. Bind off.

STRAP

With crochet hook and MC, loosely ch approx 84"/213cm. Fasten off.

FINISHING

Felting

Work in all ends before felting. Place

pieces in a zippered pillowcase and put into washing machine. Use hot-water wash and a regular (not delicate) cycle. Add ¼ cup of laundry detergent and an old towel or a pair of jeans for extra agitation. Check the pieces periodically to see if they are nice and thick and the knit stitches are no longer visible. Rinse in cold water and remove pieces from pillowcase. Shape bag, tugging on flap until desired shape and rounding the bag's bottom. You may wish to stuff with plastic bags until dry. Dry remaining pieces flat.

Appliqués

Cut square A following template A and square B following template B. Position A appliqué on flap, then whipstitch edge in place using C. Position B appliqué in center of A, then position button in center of B. Working through all thicknesses, sew button using C. Using tip of knitting needle, poke a hole in each side of bag ¾"/2cm from top edge of bag, making sure it's large enough to accommodate strap. Thread each strap end through a hole from outside to inside (tweezers will be helpful to coax end through hole). Adjust for length, knot, then trim ends to neaten.

template

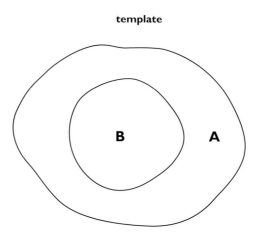

NAVAJO FELTED BAG
Southwest satchel

■■■ ▭

A traditional Navajo motif, knit in the round, graces the front of this sturdy felted bag. I-cord handles are long enough to throw over your shoulder. Designed by Bonnie Oswald.

KNITTED MEASUREMENTS
■ Approx 11"/28cm wide x 15"/38cm high x 4"/10cm deep (excluding handles)

MATERIALS
■ 4 3½oz/100g balls (each approx 220yd/201m) of Cascade Yarns *Cascade 220* (wool) in #8622 tan (MC) (4)
■ 1 ball each in #9471 brown (A), #9465 black (B), #8505 natural (C) and #9463 rust (D)
■ Two size 10½ (6.5mm) circular needles, 24"/60cm long or size to obtain gauge
■ Two size 10½ (6.5mm) double pointed needles
■ Stitch markers
■ Bobbins

GAUGE
13 sts and 18 rows to 4"/10cm over St st using 2 strands of yarn and size 10½ (6.5mm) needle (before felting).
Take time to check gauge.

Notes
1 Use 2 strands of yarn held tog throughout.
2 Bag is made in one piece.
3 When changing colors, twist yarns on WS to prevent holes in work.

BAG

Bottom
With circular needle and 2 strands of MC held tog, cast on 39 sts. Do not join. Work back and forth in garter st for 35 rows. Bind off all sts knitwise.

Body
With circular needle, 2 strands of MC held tog, and beg in center of one short side of bottom, pick up and k 9 sts evenly spaced to corner, k 39 sts along next long edge, 18 sts along next short edge, pm, 39 sts along next long edge, pm, then 9 sts along rem short edge. Beg with a p row, work back and forth in St st between two circular needles for 7 rows, end with a WS row. Change to 2 strands A and work 2 rows even. Change to 2 strands of MC and work 2 rows even.

Beg chart pat
Row 1 (RS) With 2 strands of MC, k to first marker, beg chart at st 1 and work to st 39, k to end. Cont to work chart in this way to row 39. With 2 strands of MC, work 2 rows even. Change to 2 strands A and work 2 rows even. Cont with 2 strands of MC only, purl next row.
Next (buttonhole) row (RS) K3, *bind off 2 sts, k10, bind off 2 sts, k23, bind off 2 sts, k10, bind off 2 sts*, k6, rep from * to * once more, k3.
Next row Purl, casting on 2 sts over bound-off sts. Cont in St st for 7 more rows. Bind off all sts purlwise.

HANDLES

With dpn and 2 strands of MC held tog, cast on 4 sts. Work I-cord over these 4 sts as foll: **Next row (RS)** With 2nd dpn, k3, do not turn. Slide sts back to beg of needle to work next row from RS; rep from * until I-cord measures 90"/28.5cm. Bind off.

FINISHING

Whipstitch side seam.

Felting

Work in all ends before felting. Place pieces in a zippered pillowcase and put into washing machine. Use hot-water wash and a regular (not delicate) cycle. Add ¼ cup of laundry detergent and an old towel or a pair of jeans for extra agitation. Check the pieces periodically to see if they are nice and thick and the knit stitches are no longer visible. Rinse in cold water and remove pieces from pillowcase. Shape bag to measurements. Dry pieces flat. Beg and ending at side seam, thread handle in and out of buttonholes around bag. Knot handle ends tog.

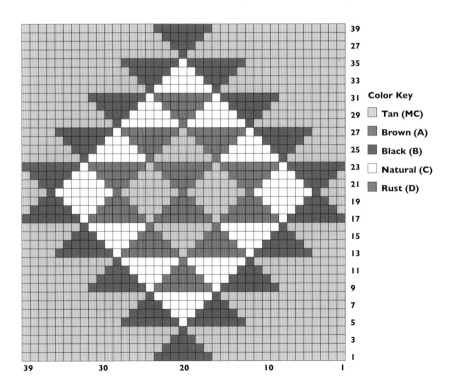

39
27
35
33
31
29
27
25
23
21
19
17
15
13
11
9
7
5
3
1

Color Key

Tan (MC)

Brown (A)

Black (B)

Natural (C)

Rust (D)

39   30   20   10   1

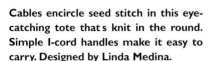

Cables encircle seed stitch in this eye-catching tote that s knit in the round. Simple I-cord handles make it easy to carry. Designed by Linda Medina.

KNITTED MEASUREMENTS
■ Approx 12"/30.5cm wide x 11"/28cm high x 3½"/9cm deep (excluding handles)

MATERIALS
■ 1 8oz/227g skein (each approx 500yd/457m) of Lorna's Laces *Fisherman* (wool) in #43ns sage (4)
■ One size 7 (4.5mm) circular needle, 24"/60cm long or size to obtain gauge
■ One set (5) size 6 (4mm) double pointed needles
■ Cable needle
■ Stitch holders
■ Stitch markers
■ One 1"/25mm button
■ ½yd/.5m lining fabric, sewing needle and thread to match
■ ½yd/.5m heavy-weight fusible interfacing
■ 3½" x 11"/9 x 28cm piece plastic needlepoint canvas

GAUGE
22 sts and 32 rnds to 4"/10cm over cable pat using size 7 (4.5mm) needle.
Take time to check gauge.

Notes
1 Bottom of bag is worked back and forth

on circular needle.
2 Body of bag is worked in the round.

STITCH GLOSSARY
6-st LC Sl 3 sts to cn and hold to front, k3, k3 from cn.
6-st RC Sl 3 sts to cn and hold to back, k3, k3 from cn.

CABLE PATTERN
(multiple of 15 sts)
Rnd 1 *P1, k4, [p1, k1] 3 times, k3, p1; rep from * around.
Rnd 2 *P1, k2, [k1, p1] 4 times, k3, p1; rep from * around.
Rnd 3 Rep row 1.
Rnd 4 Rep row 2.
Rnd 5 *P1, 6-st LC, k1, 6-st RC, p1; rep from * around.
Rnd 6 *P1, k13, p1; rep from * around.
Rnds 7—12 Rep row 6.
Rnd 13 *P1, 6-st RC, k1, 6-st LC, p1; rep from * around.
Rnd 14 Rep row 2.
Rnd 15 Rep row 1.
Rnd 16 Rep row 2.
Rep rnds 1 to 16 for cable pat.

BAG
Bottom
With circular needle, cast on 60 sts. Do not join. Work back and forth in garter st for 28 rows (14 ridges); piece should measure approx 3"/7.5cm from beg. Leave stitches on needle; do not cut yarn.

Body

With dpns and yarn from bottom of bag, pick up and k 15 sts along first short side, 60 sts along cast-on edge, then 15 sts along opposite short side—150 sts between dpns and circular needle. Pm for beg of rnd.

Next rnd Knit dropping dpns. Beg with a purl rnd, cont in garter st on circular needle for 5 rnds more. Cont in cable pat, rep rnds 1–16 5 times, then rnds 1–8 once.

Top border

Rnd 1 [P4, k7, p38, k7, p4, pm, p15, pm] twice.

Rnd 2 Knit.

Rnds 3 and 5 [P4, k7, p38, k7, p4, p15] twice.

Rnd 4 Rep rnd 2.

Rnd 6 Knit and bind off first 4 sts, ****k next 7 sts onto dpn (8 sts on needle). Work I-cord over these 8 sts as foll: *Next row (RS)** With 2nd dpn, k8, do not turn. Slide sts back to beg of needle to work next row from RS; rep from * until I-cord measures 12"/30.5cm; place sts on holder. Cut yarn and leave an 8"/20.5cm tail. Join yarn and bind off next 37 sts. K next 7 sts onto dpn (8 sts on needle). Graft sts tog (8 sts from dpn and 8 sts from holder) using Kitchener stitch, taking care not to twist I-cord.** Join yarn. Bind off next 22 sts. Rep from ** to ** once more, bind off rem 19 sts.

Block piece to measurements.

I-cord button loops

(make 2)

With dpn, cast on 3 sts. Work I-cord over these 3 sts as foll: ***Next row (RS)** With 2nd dpn, k3, do not turn. Slide sts back to beg of needle to work next row from RS; rep from * until I-cord measures 3½"/9cm. Bind off. Fold one loop half, then center between a handle, so ends extend ½"/1.3cm onto WS. Sew in place. Rep on opposite side of bag. Sew button to fold of one loop.

Lining

Cut two 14¾" x 14¼"/37.5 x 36cm pieces of interfacing. Fuse interfacing to WS of lining fabric. Cut out lining following outline of interfacing. With RS facing, sew side and bottom seams using a ½"/1.3cm seam allowance. Square bottom by folding each corner to a point. Measure 3"/7.5cm perpendicular to the seam line and mark this line. Sew across marked line. Fold corner points towards bottom and tack in place. Insert lining into bag. Fold top edge of lining to WS, so top edge of lining is ¼"/.6cm from top edge of bag. Remove lining, press fold, then topstitch ¼"/.6cm from fold all around. Cover plastic canvas with fabric. Tack to WS of bottom of lining. Insert lining back into bag. Slip stitch top edge of lining in place.

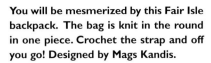

You will be mesmerized by this Fair Isle backpack. The bag is knit in the round in one piece. Crochet the strap and off you go! Designed by Mags Kandis.

KNITTED MEASUREMENTS
■ Approx 15"/38cm wide x 18"/46cm high x 3"/7.5cm deep

MATERIALS
■ 4 1¾oz/50g balls (each approx 84yd/77m) of Mission Falls *1824 Cotton* (cotton) in #100 ebony (A) 4
■ 3 balls in #103 pebble (B)
■ 1 ball in #207 chili (C)
■ One each sizes 6 and 7 (4 and 4.5mm) circular needles, 24"/60cm long *or size to obtain gauge*
■ Size G/6 (4mm) crochet hook
■ Stitch marker
■ ½yd/.5m fabric for lining, sewing needle and thread to match

GAUGE
20 sts and 22 rows to 4"/10cm over St st and chart pat using larger needle.
Take time to check gauge.

Notes
1 Bottom of bag is worked back and forth in rows on circular needle.
2 Body of bag is worked in the round.
3 Each row on chart is work from right to left.

STRIPE PATTEN
Working in St st, *2 rows A, 2 rows B; rep from * (4 rows) for stripe pat.

BAG
Bottom
With smaller needle and A, cast on 15 sts. Work back and forth in stripe pat for 70 rows. Bind off.
Body
With RS of bottom facing, larger needle and C, pick up and k 15 sts along bound-off edge, 59 sts along side edge, 15 sts along cast-on edge and 59 sts along opposite side edge—148 sts. Join and pm for beg of rnds. Purl next rnd. Drop, do not cut C.
Beg chart pat I
Rnd 1 Work 4-st rep 37 times around. Cont to work chart in this way to rnd 2. Change to C.
Next (inc) rnd Knit, inc 2 sts evenly spaced around—150 sts. Purl next rnd. Cut C.
Beg chart pat II
Rnd 1 Work 30-st rep 5 times around. Cont to work chart in this way to rnd 30, then rep rnds 1–30 twice more (90 rnds). Change to smaller needle and C.
Top border
Rnds 1 and 3 Knit.
Rnd 2 Purl.
Rnd 4 (eyelet rnd) *P13, yo, p2tog; rep from * around.

Rnd 5 Knit.
Rnd 6 Purl. Bind off.

FINISHING
Block piece to measurements.

Lining
Cut two 15½" x 20½"/39.5 x 52cm pieces of lining. With RS facing, sew side and bottom seams using a ½"/1.3cm seam allowance. Insert lining into bag. Fold top edge to WS, so edge of lining butts first rnd of top border. Slip stitch top edge of lining in place.

Strap
With crochet hook and A, ch 60"/152cm or desired length. **Row 1** Sl st in 2nd ch from hook and in each ch across. Fasten off. Beg and end at same center back eyelet, weave strap through eyelets. Knot ends of strap, then sew knots to bottom back corners.

Chart I

Chart II

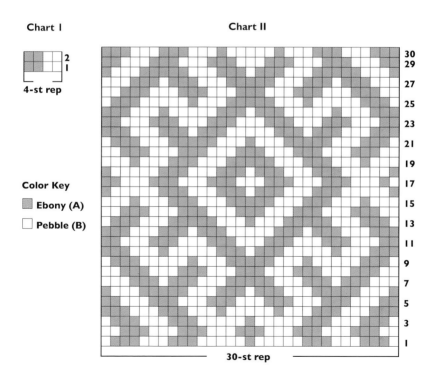

4-st rep

Color Key
■ Ebony (A)
□ Pebble (B)

30-st rep

BOTTLE BAG

Snakes on a bag

Twisted stitch cable pattern zigzags around this trendy water bottle bag. Designed by Christine Walter.

KNITTED MEASUREMENTS
■ Approx 4½"/11.5cm wide x 7"/18cm high (excluding strap)

MATERIALS
■ 1 1¾oz/50g balls (each approx 76yd/70m) of Knit One, Crochet Too *Italian Ice* (cotton/linen/viscose) in #815 banana 🔵
■ One set (5) size 6 (4mm) double pointed needles *or size to obtain gauge*
■ Cable needle
■ Stitch markers

GAUGE
20 sts and 28 rnds to 4"/10cm over St st using size 6 (4mm) dpn.
Take time to check gauge.

STITCH GLOSSARY
LPT Sl 1 st to cn and hold to front, p1, k1 tbl from cn.
LC Sl 2 sts to cn and hold to front, p1, k2 tbl from cn.
RT Sl 1 st to cn and hold to back, k1 tbl, k1 tbl from cn.
RPT Sl 1 st to cn and hold to back, k1 tbl, p1 from cn.
RC Sl 1 st to cn and hold to back, k2 tbl, p1 from cn.

BAG
Beg at top edge, cast on 48 sts. Divide sts evenly between 4 needles with 12 sts on each needle. Join, taking care not to twist sts on needle. Pm for beg of rnd and sl marker every rnd. Knit next 5 rnds.

Beg twisted st cable pat
Rnd 1 *K1 tbl, p1, LPT, p7, k1 tbl; rep from * around.
Rnd 2 *K1 tbl, p2, LPT, p6, k1 tbl; rep from * around.
Rnd 3 *K1 tbl, p3, LPT, p5, k1 tbl; rep from * around.
Rnd 4 *K1 tbl, p4, LPT, p4, k1 tbl; rep from * around.
Rnd 5 *K1 tbl, p5, LPT, p3, k1 tbl; rep from * around.
Rnd 6 *K1 tbl, p6, LPT, p2, k1 tbl; rep from * around.
Rnd 7 *K1 tbl, p7, LPT, p1, k1 tbl;, rep from * around.
Rnd 8 *K1 tbl, p8, k1 tbl, p1, k1 tbl; rep from * around.
Rnd 9 *K1 tbl, p7, RPT, p1, k1 tbl; rep from * around.
Rnd 10 *K1 tbl, p6, RPT, p2, k1 tbl; rep from * around.
Rnd 11 *K1 tbl, p5, RPT, p3, k1 tbl; rep from * around.
Rnd 12 *K1 tbl, p4, RPT, p4, k1 tbl; rep from * around.
Rnd 13 *K1 tbl, p3, RPT, p5, k1 tbl; rep from * around.

Rnd 14 *K1 tbl, p2, RPT, p6, k1 tbl; rep from * around.

Rnd 15 *K1 tbl, p1, RPT, p7, k1 tbl; rep from * around.

Rnd 16 *K1 tbl, p1, k2 tbl, p7, k1 tb;, rep from * around.

Rnd 17 *K1 tbl, p2, LC, p5, k1 tbl; rep from * around.

Rnd 18 *K1 tbl, p3, LC, p4, k1 tbl; rep from * around.

Rnd 19 *K1 tbl, p4, LC, p3, k1 tbl; rep from * around.

Rnd 20 *K1 tbl, p5, LC, p2, k1 tbl; rep from * around.

Rnd 21 *K1 tbl, p6, LC, p1, k1 tbl; rep from * around.

Rnd 22 *K1 tbl, p7, K2b, p1, k1 tbl; rep from * around.

Rnd 23 *K1 tbl, p6, RC, p1, k1 tbl; rep from * around.

Rnd 24 *K1 tbl, p5, RC, p2, k1 tbl; rep from * around.

Rnd 25 *K1 tbl, p4, RC, p3, k1 tbl; rep from * around.

Rnd 26 *K1 tbl, p4, K2b, p4, k1 tbl; rep from * around.

Rnd 27 *K1 tbl, p4, RT, p4, k1 tbl; rep from * around.

Rnd 28 *K1 tbl, p3, RPT, LPT, p3, k1 tbl; rep from * around.

Rnd 29 *K1 tbl, p3, k1 tbl, p2, k1 tbl, p3, k1 tbl; rep from * around.

Rnd 30 *K1 tbl, p3, LPT, RPT, p3, k1 tbl; rep from * around.

Rnd 31 *K1 tbl, p4, RT, p4, k1 tbl; rep from * around.

Rnd 32 *K1 tbl, p4, RT, p4, k1 tbl; rep from * around.

Rnd 33 *K1 tbl, p4, k2 tbl, p4, k1 tbl; rep from * around.

Next rnd *K1 tbl, k10, k1 tbl; rep from * around. Rep this rnd 4 times more.

Bottom shaping

Next (dec) rnd *Ssk, k to last 2 sts on dpn, k2tog; rep from * around.

Rep dec rnd 4 times more—8 sts (2 sts each needle).

Next (dec) rnd [K2tog] 4 times—4 sts. Sl sts onto one needle.

I-cord knot

Work I-cord over these 4 sts as foll: *Next row (RS)** With 2nd dpn, k3, do not turn. Slide sts back to beg of needle to work next row from RS; rep from * until I-cord measures 3"/7.5cm. Cut yarn, leaving a long tail. Thread tail in tapestry needle and weave through sts. Pull tight to gather, fasten off securely. Tie cord in a knot.

Block piece to measurements.

Twisted cord strap

(make 2)

Cut 2 strands of yarn 120"/305cm long. Fold strands in half, then knot cut ends tog. Attach knot to a fixed object. Insert a pencil into fold end. Turn pencil counter clockwise until strands are twisted tightly tog. Pull strands straight, fold in half, holding fold firmly in your right hand, then hold knotted end with pencil firmly in your left hand. Release the folded strands from your right hand, allowing all strands to twist tog. Tie ends opposite folded end in a temporary overhand knot. To attach strap, insert folded end of one twisted cord between 2 twisted rib sts and 1"/2.5cm from top edge. Untwist cord at fold, forming a loop, insert end of cord through loop, then draw through and adjust to remove slack. Rep on opposite side of back with rem strap. Unknot ends of both cords, then tie both cords tog in a firm overhand knot 2"/5cm from ends. Trim ends to neaten.

VELVET CLUTCH

Suedey pie

Simple stitches and velvety yarn give this foldover clutch its elegant appearance. Side gussets allow it to expand to hold more. Designed by Lynda Cyr.

KNITTED MEASUREMENTS
■ Approx 9"/23cm wide x 5"/12.5cm high

MATERIALS
■ 2.88oz/25g balls (each approx 63yd/ 58m) of GGH/Muench *Velour* (microfiber nylon) in #11 orange (MC) (4)
■ 1 ball in #16 lilac (CC)
■ One pair size 4 (3.5mm) needles or size to obtain gauge
■ Size E/4 (3.5mm) crochet hook
■ ½yd/.5m lining fabric, sewing needle and thread to match
■ One 12" x 18"/30.5cm x 45.5cm sheet 2mm-thick craft foam in orange

GAUGE
22 sts and 32 rows to 4"/10cm over St st using size 4 (3.5mm) needles.
Take time to check gauge.

BAG
With MC, cast on 48 sts. Work in St st until piece measures 11"/28cm from beg, end with a WS row.

Flap shaping
Next (dec) row (RS) K1, k2tog, k to last 3 sts, ssk, k1. Purl next row.

Rep last 2 rows twice more—42 sts. Purl next row. Bind off.

SIDE GUSSETS
(make 2)
With crochet hook and CC, ch 19.
Rnd 1 Work 3 sc in 2nd ch from hook (corner made), sc in next 16 ch, work 3 sc in last ch (corner made), turn to bottom lps of ch, sc in each lp across, join rnd with a sl st in first sc.
Rnd 2 Ch 1, sc in each st around, working 3 sc in center st of each corner, join rnd with a sl st in first st.
Rnd 3 Ch 1, working in back lps only, sc in each st around, working 3 sc in center st of each corner, join rnd with a sl st in first st. Fasten off.

BELT
With CC and crochet hook, ch 49.
Rnd 1 Work 3 sc in 2nd ch from hook, sc in next 46 ch, work 3 sc in last ch, turn to bottom lps of ch, sc in each lp across, join rnd with a sl st in first sc.
Rnd 2 Sl st in each st around, join rnd with a sl st in first sl st. Fasten off.
Catch
With CC and crochet hook, ch 9. Work as for belt.

FINISHING
Block pieces to measure. Using bag as a template, cut out fabric lining ½"/1.3cm

larger all around than bag and craft foam same size as bag; set aside.

Edging

With RS facing and crochet hook, join CC with a sl st in corner of cast-on edge of bag. **Rnd 1** Ch 1, making sure that work lies flat, sc evenly around entire edge, working 3 sc in each corner, join rnd with a sl st in first st. **Rnds 2–4** Sl st in each st around. When rnd 4 is completed, fasten off.

Lining

Turn fabric lining seam allowance ½"/1.3cm to WS; press. Slip stitch edge of lining to WS of bag, leaving cast-on edge of bag open. Insert foam piece; slip stitch opening closed. Sew in side gussets. On back of bag, position belt in center and so bottom edge of belt is 2"/5cm from bottom edge of bag. Sew bottom edge of belt in place, working through all thicknesses. On front of bag, position catch in center and so top edge of catch is ½"/1.3cm below bottom edge of flap. Sew each side edge of catch in place, working through all thicknesses.

FRANCINE BAG

Boho beauty

This bohemian-style bag is knit in seed stitch and trimmed with easy crochet stitches. Accent your creation with embroidered flowers, buttons and crochet beaded fringe. Designed by Margery Winter.

KNITTED MEASUREMENTS
■ Approx 18"/45.5cm wide x 13"/33cm high (excluding handles)

MATERIALS
■ 2 1¾oz/50g balls (each approx 98yd/90m) of Berroco, Inc. *Ultra Silk* (silk/rayon/nylon) in #6106 seafoam (MC) 🄴

■ 2 1¾oz/50g balls (each approx 98yd/90m) of Berroco, Inc. *Boho Colors* (nylon/cotton/rayon/polyester) in #9304 dijon (A) 🄴

■ 1 1¾oz/50g ball (each approx 98yd/90m) of Berroco, Inc. *Boho* (nylon/cotton/rayon/polyester) in #9268 pastures of plenty (B) 🄴

■ One pair size 9 (5.5mm) needles *or size to obtain gauge*

■ Size H/8 (5mm) crochet hook

■ Stitch holder

■ One pair 7½"/19cm diameter wooden ring handles

■ 1 1½"/13mm shell buttons

■ 264 6mm round glass beads with large holes

■ Sewing needle and thread

GAUGE
22 sts and 32 rows to 4"/10cm over seed st using size 9 (5.5mm) needles.
Take time to check gauge.

Notes
1 *Boho* and *Boho Colors* are self-striping yarns.
2 Back and front of bag are worked from the top down.
3 Crocheted edgings are worked after knitting is completed.

STITCH GLOSSARY
sc3tog [Insert hook in next sc, yo and draw up a lp] 3 times, yo and draw through all 4 lps on hook.

dc3tog [Yo, insert hook in next st, yo and draw up a lp, yo, draw through 2 lps on hook] 3 times, yo and draw through all 4 lps on hook.

dc2tog [Yo, insert hook in next ch-1 sp, yo and draw up a lp, yo, draw through 2 lps on hook] twice, yo and draw through all 3 lps on hook.

SEED STITCH
Row 1 (RS) *K1, p1; rep from * to end.
Row 2 K the purl sts and p the knit sts.

Rep row 2 for seed st.

BACK

Beg at top edge with MC, cast on 51 sts. Work even in seed st for 2½"/6.5cm, end with a WS row.

Beg short rows

Row 1 (RS) Work in seed st to last 5 sts, turn.

Row 2 Sl 1, work in seed st to last 5 sts, turn.

Rows 3 and 4 Sl 1, work in seed st to last 10 sts, turn.

Rows 5 and 6 Sl 1, work in seed st to last 15 sts, turn.

Rows 7 and 8 Sl 1, work in seed st to last 20 sts, turn—51 sts on needle. Mark beg and end of last row. Change to A.

First garter st band

Next (inc) row (RS) K25, M1, k1, M1, k25—53 sts. Knit next row.

Next (inc) row (RS) K25, M1, k3, M1, k25—55 sts. Knit next row.

Next (inc) row (RS) K25, M1, k5, M1, k25—57 sts. Knit next row.

Next (inc) row (RS) K25, M1, k7, M1, k25—59 sts. Knit next row. Change to MC.

Next (inc) row (RS) Knit across inc 20 sts evenly spaced—79 sts. Cont in seed st. Work even for 1 row, then bind off 2 sts at beg of next 34 rows. Bind off rem 11 sts.

Second garter st band

With RS facing and A, pick up and k 77 sts evenly spaced along entire bottom edge, beg and ending at markers; remove markers.

Next row SSK, k4, k in (front, back, front) of next st (3 sts made from 1), k6, *k3tog, k6, k in (front, back, front) of next st, k6; rep from * twice more, end k3tog, k6, k in (front, back, front) of next st, k4, k2tog—77 sts. Rep this row 7 times more, end on RS.

Next (inc) row (WS) K1, M1, k2, M1, k3, k in (front, back, front) of next st, k7, M1, *k1, M1, k7, k in (front, back, front) of next st, k7, M1; rep from * twice more, end k1, M1, k7, k in (front, back, front) of next st, k3, M1, k2, M1, k1—99 sts. Change to MC and work even in seed st for 3 rows, end with a RS row.

Next Row (WS) Working in seed St, work 18 sts, *work 2 sts tog, work 17 sts; rep from * twice more, end work 2 sts tog, work 18 sts—95 sts.

First scallop

Next row (RS) K2tog, work in seed st across next 17 sts, turn—18 sts. Place rem 76 sts onto holder for 4 more scallops. Working in seed st, dec 1 st at beg of next 15 rows. Bind off 3 rem sts.

Second scallop

With RS facing, sl 19 sts from holder onto

needle. With MC, cont to work as for first scallop.

Third, fourth and fifth scallops

Work as for second scallop.

Crocheted edging

With RS facing and crochet hook, join A with a sl st in first row of first MC scallop.

Row 1 (RS) Ch 1, *work 14 sc evenly spaced along edge of scallop to point, sc in point, work 14 sc evenly spaced to inner corner, sc in corner; rep from * 3 times more, end work 14 sc evenly spaced along edge of scallop to point, sc in point, work 14 sc evenly spaced to end—149 sc. Turn.

Row 2 Ch 4 (counts as 1 dc and ch 1), dc in first st, *[skip next st, dc in next st, skip next st, work (dc, ch 1, dc) in next st] 3 times, skip next st, work ([dc, ch 1] 3 times, dc) in next st, [skip next sc, work (dc, ch 1, dc) in next st, skip next st, dc in next st] 3 times, skip next st, sc3tog; rep from * 4 times more, end last rep work (dc, ch 1, dc) in last st instead of sc3tog. Turn.

Row 3 Sl st in first ch-1 sp, ch 3 (counts as 1 dc), work (dc, ch 1, dc) in next st, *[dc in next ch-1 sp, work (dc, ch 1, dc) in next st] twice, dc in next ch-1 sp, [work (dc, ch1, dc) in next ch-1 sp] 3 times, [dc in next ch-1 sp, work (dc, ch 1, dc) in next st] twice, dc in next ch-1 sp, dc3tog; rep from * 4 times more, end last rep work

(dc, ch 1, dc) in next st, dc in next ch-1 sp instead of dc3tog. Turn.

Row 4 Ch 4 (counts as 1 dc and ch-1), dc in first st, *[dc in next ch-1 sp, work (dc, ch 1, dc) in next st] 3 times, dc in next ch-1 sp, work ([dc, ch 1] 3 times, dc) in next ch-1 sp, [dc in next ch-1 sp, work (dc, ch 1, dc) in next st] twice, dc in next ch-1 sp, dc3tog; rep from * 4 times more, end last rep dc2tog instead of dc3tog. Turn.

Row 5 Rep row 3. Fasten off.

Handle casing

With RS facing and crochet hook, join A with a sl st in bottom of first cast-on st.

Row 1 (RS) Ch 1, sc in same st as joining, sc in bottom of next 50 sts—51 sc. Ch 1, turn.

Row 2 Sc in each st across. Ch 1, turn. Rep row 2 until casing measures approx 2 ¼"/5.5cm. Fasten off.

FRONT

Work as for back.

FINISHING

Embroidery

Cut lengths from gold section for flowers, and brown section for leaves and stems. Referring to photo, embroider a three-petal flower in center of each scallop section on bag front. Each petal has five straight stitches and the leaves also have five straight stitches. In first seed st section, a flower in center, then embroider lazy daisy stitch flowers with chain stitch stems on each side. Rep on bag back. Sew buttons on front of bag as shown in photo. Wrap each handle casing around handle to WS; sew in place. Sew front and back tog, leaving 2"/5cm unstitched each side.

Stringing beads

String 88 beads onto one strand each of MC, A and B as foll: Cut a 10"/25.5cm strand of thread and thread into sewing needle. Even up ends of thread, then make an overhand knot forming a loop. Thread end of yarn through loop. Thread bead onto needle, down thread, then down yarn.

Fringe

With RS facing, join A with a sl st in side edge of bag just before first st at bottom edge. Cont to work as foll: *Yo hook, insert hook into next st, slide 2 beads next to st, wrap yarn over left index finger, hook yarn coming from the ball and draw through st forming a 1½"/4cm loop on finger, drop loop from finger, then yo and draw through 3 lps on hook; rep from * across bottom edge, changing yarn strand each time you have completed 5 or 6 loops.

Buttons

Referring to photo, sew buttons to front of bag.

RESOURCES

Alchemy Yarns of Transformation
P.O. Box 1080
Sebastopol, CA 95473
www.alchemyyarns.com

Berroco, Inc.
P.O. Box 367
14 Elmdale Road
Uxbridge, MA 01569
www.berroco.com

Be Sweet
1315 Bridgeway
Sausalito, CA 94965
www.besweetproducts.com

Blue Sky Alpacas
P.O. Box 387
St. Francis, MN 55070
www.blueskyalpacas.com

Brown Sheep Company
100662 County Road 16
Mitchell, Nebraska 69357
www.brownsheep.com

Cascade Yarns
1224 Andover Park E.
Tukwila, WA 98188
www.cascadeyarns.com

Cherry Tree Hill
100 Cherry Tree Hill Lane
Barton, VT 05822
www.cherryyarn.com

Classic Elite Yarns
122 Western Avenue
Lowell, MA 01851
www.classiceliteyarns.com

Design Source
38 Montvale Avenue,
Suite 145
Stoneham, MA 02180

Frog Tree Yarns
14 Frog Tree Lane
East Dennis, MA 02641
www.frogtreeyarns.com

GGH
distributed by
Muench Yarns

JCA, Inc.
35 Scales Lane
Townsend, MA 01469
www.jcacrafts.com

Knit One, Crochet Too, Inc.
91 Tandberg Trail, Unit 6
Windham, ME 04062
www.knitonecrochettoo.com

La Lana Wools
136-C Paseo del Pueblo
  Norte
Taos, NM 87571
www.lalanawools.com

Lion Brand Yarn
34 West 15th Street
New York, NY 10011
www.lionbrand.com

Lorna's Laces
4229 North Honore Street
Chicago, IL 60613
www.lornaslaces.net

Louet Sales
808 Commerce Park Drive
Ogdensburg, NY 13669
www.louet.com

Manos del Uruguay
distributed by
Design Source
www.manos.com.uy

Mission Falls
100 Walnut
Door 4
Champlain, NY 12919
www.missionfalls.com

Muench Yarns, Inc.
1323 Scott Street
Petaluma, CA 94954-1135
www.myyarns.com

Nashua Handknits
distributed by
Westminster Fibers, Inc.

Reynolds
distributed by
JCA, Inc.

Skacel Collection, Inc.
PO Box 88110
Seattle, WA 98138
www.skacelknitting.com

Tahki•Stacy Charles, Inc.
70-30 80th Street
Building #36
Ridgewood, NY 11385
www.tahkistacycharles.com

Tahki Yarns
distributed by
Tahki•Stacy Charles, Inc.

Westminster Fibers
4 Townsend West, Unit 8
Nashua, NH 03063
603.886.5041
www.westminsterfibers.com

**CANADIAN
RESOURCES**

*Write to U.S. resources
for mail-order availability
of yarns not listed.*

Louet Sales
R.R. 4
Prescott, Ontario
Canada K0E 1T0
www.louet.com

Mission Falls
5333 Casgrain Ave., #1204
Montreal, Quebec
Canada H2T 1X3

Patons
320 Livingstone Avenue
    South
Listowel, ON
Canada N4W 3H3
www.patonsyarns.com

VOGUE® KNITTING BAGS TWO

Vice President,
Publisher
TRISHA MALCOLM

Editorial Director
ELAINE SILVERSTEIN

Art Director
CHI LING MOY

Executive Editor
CARLA S. SCOTT

Book Division Manager
ERICA SMITH

Graphic Designer
SHEENA T. PAUL

Associate Editor
ERIN WALSH

Yarn Editor
TANIS GRAY

Instructions Editor
CHARLOTTE PARRY

Instructions Proofreader
PAT HARSTE

Production Manager
DAVID JOINNIDES

Photography
JACK DEUTSCH STUDIO

Photo Stylist
LAURA MAFFEO

Copy Editor
KRISTINA SIGLER

▥

President,
Sixth&Spring Books
ART JOINNIDES

LOOK FOR THESE OTHER TITLES IN THE *VOGUE KNITTING ON THE GO!* SERIES...

▥